Burnout to Breakthrough

By Erin Nicole Porter

Table of Contents

1. Your Inner Child.. 24

2. The Never-ending Cycle of

    Perfectionism & Overachieving........................... 42

3. Hitting Burnout.. 54

4. Playing Small, Owning your Shit

    & Stepping into your Power................................ 67

5. I am not a Doormat...................................... 78

6. Dating, Relationships, and Sex........................... 86

7. Money & The Art of Receiving........................... 99

8. Decision Energy.. 124

9. Body Image & Burnout.................................... 136

10. Celebration & Fully Expressed.......................... 145

11. The Breakthrough.. 155

Dedication

This book is dedicated to my Grandma, Sandra Bowerman. She was so excited to know that I was writing a book and fulfilling my lifelong dream. I miss you daily and thank you for the endless hummingbirds you send my way as a sign I am on the right path.

Mom - Thank you for always being my cheerleader over the years, since I was a little girl you always encouraged me to follow my dreams and to do the things that didn't make "sense" to others and to follow my heart. You are always my sounding board and I love you so much. **Aj** - you are one of my greatest cheerleaders too, thank you for coming into our family and always being so proud of me!

Dad, I always appreciate your long life chats even if I give you a hard time for them. Thank you for always pushing me to keep going and to trust myself and to never sellle.

Carla - So glad you were brought into my life as well and thank you for the laughs and connection always!

Jason, Matt, Adam & Sarah - Even though you all drive me crazy...(minus Sarah LOL) deep down you are the lovingest brothers and supporters in my life. Thanks for making me strong and always supporting my journey! **Sarah** - thank you for coming in to save me and being the sister I always wanted!

Autumn, Trent, Aubrey, & Emma - Thank you sweet ones for always making my day brighter, I love you little munchkins and wish I could see you more! So proud of each of you.

Nik - Hard to believe accidentally jumping on your zoom call years ago led to one of the best friendships I've ever had in my life. I cannot thank you enough for being an amazing big sister to me, for supporting me on this journey, listening to my crazy messages of life, and writing the foreword to this book. You are my otter.

Lily - Aunt Lily girl, what would I do without you? I really have no fucking idea and that is the truth. From being my client to one of my best friends, I am so grateful for you every day and thank you for always being one I can lean on, drink rose with, and give unwelcomed hugs to.

Melissa - One of the most powerful and humble women I know. Thank you for guiding me and being a safe space for me to always land, encouraging me, and for all the deep belly laughs.

Sam - My little gingersnap. You were there for the beginning when I said, I'm finally going to write this thing and cheered me on every single day. Thank you for being the fire in my life, keeping me healthy, and reminding me to always express my heart.

Troy- Thanks for not minding me waking up at 6am these last few months to write so early in the morning! So glad you were brought into my life!

Natalie - Thank you for always holding the safest space for me, honest friendship conversations, and being able to fully speak my truth and provide such deep support. Imagine a salem GIF in love.

Kelli - I love you with all my heart, thank you for always being there no matter what, holding me in my healing journey and being a rock in my life!

Lauren A. - My beautiful projector guide, thank you for seeing me so deeply, celebrating me always, and always encouraging me to keep going!

Lauren M. - It was weird to write M instead of P. From 2nd grade on you've always cheered me on and made a point to see me always. Your support, your love, and your constant celebrations for me, mean the world to me. I love you!

Leah - From the days of Kindergarten bracelets, to weddings, and everything in between, so grateful to have you as my best friend all these years!

Marci - Your beautiful book and ability to go for it gave me so much inspiration. I will truly cherish our Sedona trip, your love, and my forever peacock dusta sista.

Kelsey - My first book writing and play buddy, thank you for always allowing me to use you as my dummy in all the crazy inspirational ideas I had in my younger years. Love you!

Steph - thank you for the endless giggles, moscow mules, and expression of my desires, love you!

Mick - thank you for the years of roomie vibes, support, and cheering me on. I love and miss you so much!

My Clients - You all are the reason I am here today. I am so proud of all of you and thank you all deeply for supporting me, cheering me on, and helping me become a better coach and leader every single day. I love you all so much past and present.

My team - I couldn't have done this without each and every single one of you, from graphic design to support on all the things BTS, to editing, I am in awe and so blessed to have such an amazing support system.

Online Coach Friends - to those of you who have been with me through the beginning and those I met along the way, I love you!

Energetics of Business Community - What an incredible podcast community, thank you for supporting me and listening on this journey.

QRE Community - My heart and soul. It's an honor to coach and support you all on your journey to deepening your craft and changing the field of coaching. So proud of you all.

Andrew - I truly cannot begin to thank you enough for the depths you have been able to support me through in my healing journey. Thank you for changing my life, being one of the biggest inspirations I have ever known, and always supporting me to the depths. This healing journey wouldn't be possible without you and I am forever grateful for your mentorship!

Anthony - Thank you all for the support and being such an incredible mentor to me, I wouldn't be here without you! You truly impacted my life.

Melanie E. - My spiritual guide and mentor, thank you for inspiring me to always go after it, for bringing the channeling through for this book, and always being my number one hype woman.

Jen Casey - I wouldn't be here without you, thank you for being an incredible first coach of mine and encouraging me every step of the way!

Extended Family - Thank you all for the love and support!

My Childhood Friends (Lauren, Leah, Alexa, Paige, Maggie) - Thank you all for always being the FAB 5 and such amazing supporters along the way!

My California Friends - You all are a dream come true, I love all of our nights together and healing days!

BG Friends & Alpha Phi Sisters - The mentorship, connection, fun times and support through the years has always meant the world. I am so grateful for you all!

Britt M. - Miss you my love, thank you for always being there for the deepest support through the years!!

Molly - I love you G! Thank you for always cheering me on.

Spirit Team - Thanks for all the channeled downloads, you all are the real MVPs here.

Book Design by Keisha Jordan

Editing and Formatting by Alecia Harris

Copyright 2021

How This Book Works

This book is infused with my own personal stories and reflections, followed by an integration lesson and/or embodiment practices. As I always say in my coaching sessions. Take what works for you and leave what doesn't feel right in your body. These are my experiences, thoughts, and reflections. Practicing discernment in your healing journey is so important. Asking yourself, is this a yes for me or is this a no for me? Start connecting into as you read this book, the body sensations that pop up. I share vulnerable information and experiences which may trigger certain emotions and reactions in your body. Practice holding yourself as any of these things come through and as always, reach out to a healthcare or mental health professional if you need support as I am not a doctor nor am I a replacement for any of those things. I also acknowledge my privilege as a white heterosexual woman as I write this book and knowing my lens impacts how I've navigated through life.

Foreward

When I think of Erin, the first thing that comes to me is a feeling. A feeling that envelopes my being. A feeling of safety. Calmness. Softness. A feeling of true authenticity and comfort in *being*. I have never met another human more comfortable with simple *being* in my life than Erin Nicole Porter.

The journey coming home to yourself is a wild ride. To unmask and undo all that created your very identity in the first place requires a brave soul. To strip away all protections and walls that once kept us safe. To get comfy with our emotions and look at and accept all of our not-so-pretty shadows. It requires a level of vulnerability and intimacy with the Self like we've never experienced before.

Erin came into my life just when I needed her most. I had just started my coaching business and was navigating the rat race of being an entrepreneur. We both bonded instantly being new to this world and found comfort in each other's "weird". She instantly became the best friend I didn't know I needed on that part of my journey. There's an energetic innocence about this time for the both of us that will forever and always hold a special place in our heart as we continue to grow and navigate this human experience, sometimes together and sometimes apart.

Back then, Erin quickly became my health coach and became Erin's personal growth & love coach. In my first session with Erin, I instantly saw a beautiful girl that hid behind a smile. She was so gorgeous inside and out and yet still felt the need to prove herself to the world and earn love.

As she describes in the first chapter of the book, I was the coach that first introduced her to "Little E". Her inner child. I will never forget the moment she realized this little girl was still with her as tears streamed down her beautiful, porcelain face. At the time, she saw tears as a weakness. She found pride in her ability to not feel and instead push through. She wanted solutions. She didn't come to me to "feel" and that pissed her off at first.

Erin quickly found *feeling* to be her way out. She started to become comfortable with her emotions and started to find safety in surrender rather than control. She began to let go and step more into pleasure rather than the hustle that she was so used to. She came back home to Little E and gave her everything that she needed as a little girl that was missed.

I may have been the catalyst that started Erin on her journey back home to her most authentic self, but it certainly didn't stop there. I watched Erin take what she learned and run with it. She found mentor after mentor that could support her more deeply the deeper she went with herself. She took all the trainings, read all the books and integrated and embodied them all. This became her life mission.

Erin has finally found home within herself. She no longer looks for outside validation and safety from men, success or money and instead validates her own self just in the pure essence of who she truly is. The part that will never die when the identity of Erin Nicole Porter leaves earthside.

You see, we are all in this race to achieve. To get the next shiny thing to finally feel enough. To finally feel worthy. What Erin teaches in the book is that your worthiness is found in the exact essence of the energy and consciousness of who you truly are. That energy from which you were created from to begin with. In the eternal part of you that will live on forever. When we can peel back the layers of who we think we are from our own childhood, we start to tap into this exact innate worthiness I am referring to here. Your identity is not fixed. It is always evolving. By returning back home to your most authentic state, you will arrive at a remembrance of that worth. Of your enoughness. Constantly proving yourself creates the burnout. That is what the following pages of this book are all about. How to arrive at your own *breakthrough*.

I am honored to have been asked to write this for Erin. I asked her why she chose me and she said, "Wouldn't be here without ya." But truth is, I wouldn't be where I am today without her for more reasons than she even realizes. She has been my motivation and source of power silently watching from afar without her knowing it. I may be older than Erin, but Erin has taught me what it is like to be in my power. To no longer live my own life as the "best kept secret" that I used to pride myself on and instead fully harness my own innate worthiness and power. Erin is a force to be reckoned with...literally. She may be gentle but she is powerful beyond measure and just being in her energy from this book will give you that same taste of your own power that she has given me through the years.

I love you my little sis...I know this is just the beginning for you and can't wait to celebrate you every step of the way! Xoxo

Nikki Amaturo
Inner Child Specialist & Spiritual Teacher

Introduction

When I started Kindergarten I had 3 goals. I wanted to tie my shoes, ride my bike without training wheels, and blow a bubble with bubblegum. Ever since my young age I was programmed to see how much I could do at one time. Take on one (or ten) goals, accomplish it, onto the next. There was never a moment to truly celebrate what I had accomplished. I needed to continue onto the next thing, the next thing, and the next.

I defined my worthiness by how much I could do, how much I could achieve, and how successful I could be. I brought an energy to my life that let me build and accomplish to earn love, and to run away from what I wanted instead of running towards a desire.

Did I realize I was doing this consciously? Of course not, but the power of your subconscious mind is incredible. We do most of the things in our life on autopilot. We go from one thing to the next, without recognizing or celebrating ourselves along the way.

I found pride in the hustle, in the word "busy", in the energy of chasing. Slowing down, relaxing, receiving was not in my vocabulary. I soon found it was the biggest cockblock of receiving abundance, love, and connection in my life - because I couldn't fully open myself up to receive. I operated in the realm of the doing. Unconsciously, this is where I felt safe. This is how I earned love, felt worthy, and could control my surroundings.

When people talked about feeling safe to slow down - I nodded my head. *"Yes, sure I can slow down, it feels safe to receive."*

My conscious mind wanted to repeat the affirmations, the journal prompts, and the smile on my face, but internally my whole body and internal responses were freaking out. Later on in the book, I'll dive deeper in how I began to truly understand, heal my system and how I found the ability to slow down and feel safe and supported.

Most of my life I operated in the linear of the doing. If I could work harder, do more, effort my way into who I wanted to become, then the magic would happen.

I achieved so much, which I am so proud of myself for, but my message here in this book to you is a little different. It's to help all of us change the paradigm of needing to work harder, to burn ourselves out in order to earn more, to end the cycle of being busy, and to stop feeling like we have to prove and push our way through life.

When I learned about the concept of Be, Do, Have - I realized I had so much of my life backwards. I always thought to myself, once I have a certain income level, the perfect relationship, then I can do xyz, and become the woman I'm wanting to be!

Eek, wrong.

I interpreted *doing* with *earning*. I strategized my business and my life to a T. Everything had a game plan, everything had been reverse engineered. I lived in the do.

When I started to focus on who I was going to become, my life shifted. I started to bring awareness to the mentality of *"I am a person who does something."* Not someone who **does something to become a person.** I can embody that version of me now and take action from that place.

So this book is for you. The woman who is ready for the next breakthrough. The woman who is ready to stop getting in her own way, who is tired of being a best kept secret, or not having all of the pieces of her life she desires. To the woman who is ready to step into her power, own her gifts, celebrate, enjoy pleasure, excitement, and ease.

Welcome to Burnout to Breakthrough.

This book is broken up into a mix of my story, my lessons, my burnout and my breakthrough moments. At the end of each chapter there are journal prompts and integration practices so you can begin to dive into your own healing and uncover different areas of your life. In addition, there's an online course with tools such as EFT, breathwork, hypnosis, & meditations to support you in this work. You can find this on my website: www.erinnicolecoaching.com/breakthrough

Oh ya, I guess I should tell you who I am. I'm Erin. Sometimes I find it hard to describe the blend of all the things I do. I'm a Business Alchemist, aka a Business Mentor with a Focus in Business Energetics and Aligned Business Strategy. I'm a Master Practitioner & Trainer of NLP & Hypnosis, EFT, a Breathwork Facilitator, Somatic Experiencing Practitioner, Adult Attachment Repair Model Therapist, Reiki Master Teacher, and host of The Energetics of Business Podcast.

I enjoy and excel in coaching women in facilitating quantum transformation through my coaching certification: The Quantum Ripple Effect. I also teach women how to heal internally so their businesses can thrive, and teaches them aligned business strategy and CEO Embodiment.

After spending years in my hustle and go-go high achieving energy, I found the less perfection I embraced, the more I let go and surrendered and ran my business from the soul, the more my business to skyrocketed to now consistent multiple six figure years.

I help women embrace their play, pleasure, and power to increase their sales, heal, and understand the energetics of business. My clients have gone on to become multiple six figure coaches, international speakers, authors, and have had incredible internal healing and transformation.

I have a Masters in Education, backgrounds in Crisis Management, Student Development, and Marketing and spent time as a health and fitness coach before stepping into the mindset and business world. I live in San Diego, CA with my two puppies Maizey & Ziggy, but I am a country girl from small-town Ohio at heart. www.erinnicolecoaching.com

PS, if you want to save on our Burnout to Breakthrough mini program that comes with the book, use the code BREAKTHROUGH at checkout.

Chapter 1: Your Inner Child

"Whose love did you feel you had to earn more?"

Thank you to Nikki Amaturo, my past relationship coach and best friend for asking me this question several years ago. Cue sobbing. The beginning of my journey with inner child work, was the opening to my doors of "holy shit my little girl needs support."

Honestly, I was not ready for the depth of this work that would soon change my life. I thought I had done so much mindset work and personal development. However, I quickly realized something along the way. Personal development and the straight up HEALING work - are two different worlds apart.

I didn't think I needed "mindset," I needed strategy for my business and relationships. I needed the how and the way. As you can see, this beautiful woman wrote the foreword for this book, but honestly I was pissed at her during our first session.

"He's either going to come along with you, or he's not."

I thought to myself..what? I came to you for help in my relationship and to (what I thought at the time was to) fix it. Back then, I was constantly looking for the way and the how to get through something in my life.

Oh boy, was I wrong. I fought back the tears at the time she asked me that question about my little girl. She told me: It's okay to cry. You don't have to be perfect or have it all together here.

Cue more sobbing.

That was my little girl. The little version of Erin who wanted to be perfect. She wanted to make everyone around her happy. Her little empathic self couldn't stand to have anyone upset with her. She would put everyone else around her first in order to please the masses (see: I am not a doormat chapter). She followed the rules, cried her eyes out when she got her first B on a paper, and stayed very quiet in hopes that if she didn't speak her mind everyone would love her.

I was loved. Inside however, was turmoil. I wanted to speak up, speak my truth, but "keep quiet" and "put your head down" and "if you don't have anything nice to say, don't say anything at all" was taken to the extreme in my body. I felt fear and didn't feel supported in ever rocking the boat or speaking up for what I needed emotionally. Instead, I took on the roll of care-taking for everyone and everything in my life. By meeting other people's needs I could bypass my own needs and find fulfillment in that cycle.

I was applauded all my life for my successes. I was extremely hard on myself. I hid a lot of the times I felt upset because it wasn't "that" bad. I had to keep going. I stuffed down my emotions, my needs, and my experiences because I didn't want to bother anybody else. I could handle it all on my own, or so I thought.

Side note: anytime in the book I refer to Little Erin, or Little E, I'm referring to my inner child. Also, I cuss a lot in this book so if that offends you, now would be the time to close this book.

Little Erin (before the place of "doing") was a wild child. She wore ice cream buckets on her head, was bossy to her brothers, had a wild imagination, and to be quite honest - gave no fucks. Little Erin followed me to every area of my life. That overachiever, must have it all together mentality, began to burn me out before I could even recognize what was happening. She believed everything had to be hard. **Hard** was connected to worthiness. **Hard** meant it was enough.

What I began to realize, longer down my journey, is that this was all unconscious blueprinting and trauma. Of course I "consciously" didn't want things to be hard, but it was how I felt loved, how I felt safe.

My body knew the programming of hustle - do all the things, burn out, have zero boundaries, but it didn't feel safe to let things be easy. I had hit burnout so many times in my life it left me hospitalized with chronic symptoms, panic attacks, anxiety, and so many other things.

Here's the thing. Our unconscious mind runs 99.999996% of our programming. This means, we are basically operating on autopilot most of our days. 2.3 million bits of information/second comes into our awareness and we can only process 126 bits consciously. That is a huge difference. So our bodies and our minds are sponges for what we are soaking in.

We soak things in (in a big way) before the age of 7. We also soak in things from past lives, our time in the womb, and generationally. Generational trauma can be passed in DNA as well. Trauma can be passed down. And guess what? So can healing.

You might be thinking to yourself, but I didn't have a "bad childhood" or grow up in a home with a lot of chaos. Honestly, I didn't either. It still doesn't mean as unique individuals that we didn't get our needs met the way we needed them to be met. Our parents, or caregivers, can do the best they can with what they know and it still might not be able to meet our needs energetically.

Also, remember - what might not have been traumatic for one person, may have been extremely traumatic for the next. Our body somatically stores memories which is why it doesn't always "make sense."

My little girl, little E, had a hard time receiving. She wanted to do it all herself. She had a lot of pride in wanting to not ask for help which meant she was blocking herself from receiving.

So let's talk about the concept of receiving energy.

Many of my clients come to me wanting support in deepening their capacity to receive. I believe receiving energy happens in layers. There is a cycle of awareness of receiving, feeling safe to receive, opening ourselves up to receive, allowing it into our body, keeping, having, and re-creating the overflow of receiving.

Let's break this down further.

The first concept is understanding there is an energy to receive. We often block even the smallest forms of receiving: compliments, help, support. I know I did. I had a belief that no one could meet me where I needed to be met at and it was safer to do it all myself. It felt better to justify a compliment or over-explain myself on why I needed support.

I remember one time asking my Dad for money and having a full on panic attack. Back then, asking for help meant I didn't have it all together, it wasn't okay to receive and from there came massive shame, guilt, and fear.

The first stepping stone is allowing yourself to receive support and feeling safe in your body to do so. Really holding your body as you receive. Letting the compliment, the money, the opportunity, the support come in and feel how it feels to receive it.

For me it was helpful to start with: *Thank you, I receive that.*

Feeling safe to receive can be a deep unconscious blueprint in our system and often based on past traumas as well. For many, it doesn't feel safe to receive. It didn't for me either. Receiving is a state of being and being (resting, allowing, the feminine) wasn't safe. In this state I would question "how do I prove my worth here" or "what if I get bored" "what if, what if, what if…"

The programming to go, go, go and do all the things feels safer for most of us. We know how to operate here. I always knew how to operate in the highs and how to operate in the lows. So I consistently brought those energies into my life.

It felt known in my body to ride a roller coaster of good things happen and then bad things happen. My body didn't feel safe in keeping and truly having my desires and what it is I was receiving, because I was constantly waiting for the other shoe to drop.

I watched the other shoe drop so many times: in business, in relationships, in life, you name it. I was almost more addicted to the struggle life brought than in the ease.

Healing was the next layer, and that meant being able to sit in an energy of well-being, and in a place of keeping and having. I had to work daily to re-encode the belief that it wasn't going to be taken away from me, that I wouldn't get left behind, that it was safe to be in overflow. This was beginning to deeply regulate my nervous system, my unconscious mind, and the sensations in my body. I would begin to notice where I was scanning for something to happen or holding myself back from wanting more in case it didn't show up. I'll share more about the practices I use to support myself in this later on.

Here's the thing, our little person is running so much of our adult life. This is why it's important to dive into the inner work, the healing work, and our parts and protectors that are keeping us safe. Our little person shows up in our businesses, relationships, in friendships and so much more.

Throughout childhood we develop strategies, protectors, and mechanisms to help keep us safe. We implement these different patterns and when they work, we keep them and if they don't work, we attempt to find new strategies. We develop parts of us, as we grow, that take on different roles. Some of these roles we develop are for safety, for getting needs met, and for protection.

What I help my clients do, and what helped myself in inner child work, is getting our adult to meet our inner child. It's about getting them online together so the inner child can do the healing work he/she/they needs in order to operate in our current reality.

Often, our caregivers or parents were doing the best they could with the resources they knew at the time, but we also as children have different needs that couldn't be expressed, which means our caregivers couldn't meet us where we needed to be met either emotionally, physically, mentally, etc.

This is where we might begin to either meet our own needs, rely on others to meet our needs, project our needs onto others, attempt to fix, rescue, push through, bypass, or search around for partners or friends to meet our needs. We spend so much of our lives looking outside of ourselves to meet what it is we want, instead of looking internally, or vice versa.

What's the benefit to being able to learn how to meet and receive our needs? When we can meet our own needs, heal our little person, and begin to feel fulfilled internally, we stop reaching outside of ourselves to bring in a missed experience. Then, we also get to have other people, experiences, etc. meet our needs too.

However, when the external need is coming in and we receive this, it's operating in a space of overflow rather than filling up our cup. We are whole and worthy internally, just as we are, every single day.

We also get needs met by others too (healthily of course). We receive from the self, receive from others, receive from a group, and receive from spirit/God/Universe whatever you choose to connect to. One of these often presents an edge.

We might find that it's easy to receive from ourselves. This might look like giving ourselves a self-care day, doing something for ourselves, meeting our own needs. Receiving from another is allowing someone to hold us when we're open, to support us (maybe a partner, a team member) and receiving from a group might be allowing a sisterhood of people to support you, or feeling into the energy of a mastermind or whatever it might be.

When I say one of these presents an edge it means that one of these opens us up to a vulnerability or a discomfort to grow through.

For me, it first started as being able to receive from another. The vulnerability and openness was difficult, then with time I could open up more. Then allowing myself to be held and open in a group of people (that were safe of course) presented new edges to work through.

I love working with all three because it presents so much in our ability to deepen our energetic capacity to receive. It allows us to receive more love, abundance, connection, support, and wellbeing overall in every area of our lives. In your conscious mind you might be thinking, well of course I want to receive and not run these patterns or beliefs. Remember, 99.99996% of our thoughts are running on autopilot, happening through our subconscious mind. This means, we are taking in thoughts, beliefs and energies of everyone around us. We take in beliefs & experiences in the body from past life experiences, generational experiences, and womb experiences. That is why it's so important for us to heal this for those who have come before us and those who will come after us.

INTEGRATION & EMBODIMENT:

How to Begin to Connect in with Your Inner Child & Help Support her/how you identify.

Everything in life starts with awareness. Take a moment to meet in with your inner child each day. Ask them, what are you needing from me today? If you find yourself in a trigger, asking yourself how can I support you and allow you to feel safe to move through this?

I also like to use my FIRES method, which you find more of inside of my mini program: Burnout to Breakthrough.

F: Feel. How can I bring my awareness to this emotion that I am feeling? Allow yourself to be with the emotion, to hold yourself and take a breath and allow the compassion to flood through your body as you experience what is coming up for you. You might explore where the emotion is coming up in your body, if it has a texture, a sensation (positive, neutral, negative) and be with it. A mentor once said to me it's like feeling the weather vs. reporting about the weather.

I: Integrate. In the integration we begin the awareness process. You might explore the pattern and the feeling, where else in life you may have felt this way, if it's a response to an old pattern or feeling, or a fact to what's happening In this moment. As you move forward you also can bring your awareness to integrate what might be coming through for you and how the body wants to respond, what you may want to say, or what is coming through.

*R: **Reprogram & Reparent.** Depending upon the situation and the experience, these are some of the questions I will use as a guide to begin to reprogram the belief or make change moving forward to something that might have come up. Not all of these may be applicable, but they are great questions to use to process. The reprogramming comes from following through once you find more answers to these questions.*

- How can I see this differently?
- How can I hold space?
- What does my little girl need?
- What does this part need?
- How am I choosing to respond?
- What message do I need to share with this part of me, or protector?
- What's the frequency or need that needs to be met?

E: Embodying. Embodying is all about taking the information from a knowing, to an integration, to embodying it. Embodying who it is we desire to be, what it is we are stepping into, and where it is we desire to go is a beautiful way to take all of this work one step deeper. Again, these are a variety of questions to guide you and not all of FIRES might be applicable in a specific scenario.

- How can I embody this next level?
- How can I allow myself to be with my current experience?
- Bring compassion into this experience
- How is my highest self showing up?
- What would it look like to drop out of my mind and drop into my body?
- Taking deep breaths, placing hands over those parts that the pressure is feeling and meeting the need..what is it that you need right now?

S: Surrender. Surrender is all about releasing the constant need to control, to know, to consciously *understand. It's about releasing the pressure, the way we think it's supposed to be, the how, and detaching from the outcome. This process is hard to do without a foundation of feeling safe and supported in our systems. The ego always loves to control, to know how, to figure out the why to keep us safe. It's a beautiful protector and we don't want to make it wrong or bad, we want to honor it as it has kept us safe for so long. Affirming: it's safe to trust yourself. Some questions to take with you:*

- Where can I let go and surrender?
- How can I trust myself and my intuition?
- Where am I trying to control the outcome/the how?

Journal Prompts:

- What did you feel you needed to do in order to receive love?
- Who did you have to earn more love from?
- What beliefs is your little person still holding onto?
- What are the needs of your little person?

- How can you honor your little person throughout the day & check in with what is coming up for her?

Remember, she is the one that navigates so much of our day to day. She will show up in relationships, in life, in business, in friendships until we help her feel supported and to continue growing up in her patterns. Be gentle on her and attune to her the way you would a child.

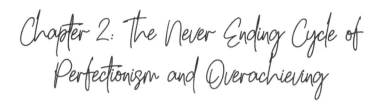

Chapter 2: The Never Ending Cycle of Perfectionism and Overachieving

I realized perfectionism kept me stuck most of my life.

Ever since I was a little girl I found my worthiness in how much I could have my shit together and what I could achieve. For me, it's what kept me going. It kept me in avoidance of the feelings I didn't want to have to feel.

I put on a face of being happy and positive all the time. It was a way to protect myself from having to actually sit and feel the emotions that would come through. If I could just act okay on the outside, that meant I had it all together. If it appeared that I had it all together, I wouldn't have to be vulnerable and no one would see that I was slowly struggling inside.

Perfectionism kept me safe, it kept me small, and it kept me quiet. I had a deep desire for everyone to like me, for everyone to be my friend. I didn't want to rock the boat, to upset people, or to let them down. I avoided conflict like the plague. I needed everyone to like me in order to feel enough in my life.

We all have these beautiful gifts called protectors. Protectors are parts of us that got stuck in our consciousness, somewhere on our life's journey, and they are meant to keep us safe. They are fragments of our inner child and at some point, or many points, they had to run a certain strategy in order to keep us safe. They are strong and incredible and have beautiful gifts when they are operating in their embodied selves. When we can get them connected with our adult form, the healing begins to happen.

Imagine as if your adult is a friend to the protector state. They have to befriend the protector, find out what "need" it needs to be met, what it's afraid of, and how to support it so it can feel safe to go deeper into the healing work. One of my protectors is the achiever. She wants to come online to keep me going, keep me safe, and she protected me from having to deeply feel certain experiences In my lIfe. She also helped me take care of others and make sure others were always okay. However, this often came at the expense of taking care of myself.

As I've learned to attune to her in a healthy adult presence, and as I've had to meet her in so many ways she didn't get met growing up, she began to feel safe to let more come through and more open up in my life. As one of my mentors, Andrew, shared with me once, "no parts get left behind," which really resonated with me. These parts don't get left behind in our healing journey, they grow with us and we get to work with their gifts.

You might reflect on what protectors come up for you. Maybe it's a part who blended in to keep the peace, a part who resists connection, whatever she may be, I invite you to begin to connect with her and see where there is to explore with your relationship to the parts of you.

One of the things that was always so hard for my achiever part was celebration. There was never a celebration of the successes along the way. I lived in the more I could do, the more I could achieve, the more I could earn, the more I could be loved and seen. I lived in a place of what I now call the linear: **doing to receive.** I would bypass my success. I could get Straight A's, all the accolades, scholarships, and everything there was, but to me it was never enough. There was "no point" to celebrate because there was so much more to do.

I began to learn about celebration from a beautiful mentor of mine, Jen Casey, but honestly wasn't ready to hear it when she first told me about it. We got on a call to plan out my launch and she said lets celebrate it! In my head I was like: wtf Jen, I haven't even put this shit out there yet, help me with my funnel. She told me I should book a celebration dinner, and we should get up and celebrate and dance on the call. I did not want to do those things. There was work to do and I felt so awkward being seen, dancing, and celebrating something that I couldn't get behind energetically that I thought might not happen.

I felt those feelings so much growing up. I didn't want to do anything silly in front of people in fear of what would be said about me. I would get internal anxiety about all of this. Yet, I could speak in front of people no problem. The second it went personal, I felt so much judgment in my head. What are they thinking, what are they saying, how am I being perceived?

Achieving, for me, was similar to a high. I liked the feeling of success, the feeling of crossing something off my checklist, but the problem was: it was never enough.

It never felt enough to me. I was waiting for one day, to be the thing, the thing that would change everything. I began to understand that I could collapse time by feeling and embodying the energy of my celebrations, where it is I desired to go, and the things I wanted to call in for my life. If I could feel those things and create them into my reality before they were here, I could align myself with the vibration of it and begin to call it into my physical world.

This is the magic of quantum leaping. It worked for me in celebrating, practicing pure gratitude, allowing myself to own my power, my celebrations, my success and actually internally celebrating that feeling I felt, rather than by passing it.

When we bypass our celebrations, or say when I...then I will...it will always feel never enough. In the eyes of source/universe/creator/God, It's hard for them to give you more when you aren't grateful for what you currently have. I had to start owning my own celebrations and not just use others to give me that gratitude. It had to come from within.

Little Erin needed that love, that celebration, that gratitude she never gave herself. However, I found myself in the earlier stages of truly tapping into celebrations, that I replaced my little girl's wishes for someone to see her and celebrate her - with her coaches. I would feel validated when they could celebrate me and felt enough. I was re-enacting that trauma response by getting their validation and external celebration. Boom. It hit me. This was happening again. It's one thing to have someone celebrate you and hold that space, but what was happening for a while was that I was doing it in order to feel enough for them too. The next layer of healing was here. She had to quit running, quit chasing, and begin to find that feeling within.

I love to explore celebrations from both internal celebrations and external celebrations. Internal celebration for me comes as more of an internal and felt sense of feeling. It's leaning into the goodness, the well-being, and marinating in the magic. It's honoring myself, where I've been, where I'm going and being present to the stillness of what I am celebrating. I anchor this sensation to my body and allow myself to fully soak in the moments. External celebration may be more outwardly expressed. It's sharing a celebration, taking up space, going to treat myself somehow, and honoring my physical body. I embody the celebrations first before outwardly sharing.

There's so many ways we can practice internal and external celebration and gratitude. The more we celebrate who we are, what we've done, and our essence of our being, the more of that we attract our way.

Speaking of essence. Here is a question I want you to reflect on. ***How often were you celebrated for who you were as a child, not just your achievements or what you were doing, but truly your identity, your being, your internal state?***

Remember this: Your desires are meant to be yours. Your celebrations now snowball into future celebrations. When we live in a world of "when this happens - then I'll do the thing," or "I'll celebrate when it's the BIG goal," we miss the magic and the journey along the way. We miss the divine timing and the unfolding of our journey of life. We find ourselves gripping and grasping at a goal or outcome thinking that the income, the relationship, the career goal, or whatever it is will be the thing that changes everything. Then we get there and we realize that it was a false sense of validation.

It's great to have big goals and big desires, OF COURSE! But truly, take a moment and ask yourself. What internal feeling do I think that is going to bring in when I get it? Do I think having more money will make me free and feel safe? Sure, there's more options when you're financially free and things you can do. However, I promise you those goals can be bandaids thinking that as it comes in, things will shift.

Things shift now. You can heal the searching for validation and create the state you want to feel and then you magnetize what you desire to you.

Think that more money will bring you safety? How can you heal internally so you can create safety in your body now?

Think that more followers will bring you more opportunities to be seen? How can you see yourself now and heal the parts of you that weren't seen over the years?

Think that when you get the relationship that your world will change? How can you create those things you want in a partner now and heal past programming as a child and with previous partners?

When you go first, the universe will always respond to your vibration, your healing, your essence.

Sometimes, it's going to be messy and it will make zero sense. You're not here for average if you're reading this book though. You're here for the things that make zero fucking sense. You're here to say yes to you, your goals, your desires and allow yourself to be met in them along the way. Waiting until things are perfect, the timing is right, or whatever it is to leave the job, the relationship... is waiting on potentiality. You get to create this new reality you desire for yourself. Take messy action, jump, trust yourself so deeply and know that you're always learning and growing along the way.

INTEGRATION & EMBODIMENT:

Who are we if we aren't achieving?

Most of our lives we are spent moving away, towards, through, or with something to get through, get to, get over, or get with it.

Don't get me wrong, healthy achievement is needed. Our unconscious mind is literally programmed for us to "keep wanting more" and for most of us, it has helped us meet needs inside of us and some that weren't met as we were growing up.

My question for you is how often do you take time in the now?

In the present.

In the stillness.

In the pure celebration.

In the surrender.

Awareness of the beauty of what is.

To really feel. (and feeling from the body, not reporting what the body is feeling from the mind)

There's a deep sense of well-being, joy, pleasure, ease, and beauty when we can honor where we are on the journey, rather than running, numbing, chasing (which are all beautiful protection strategies we've used for so long) and there's so much more we can do when we work with them from an embodied state. I'll invite you to sit with that. What's it feel like for you to be fully present? Are you focused on anchoring the moment or scanning for what's next?

- How are you currently celebrating your success?
- How can you celebrate yourself for who you are and your essence?
- Are you finding yourself in a chase or running/searching for the next thing?

Take a day this week to fully celebrate you. Maybe it's going out to dinner, buying yourself a coffee, or maybe even running a bath and listing out in your journal everything you want to celebrate about yourself. Want another challenge? Ask someone you love, and that you feel safe with, to hold space for you as you celebrate yourself and have them reflect it back to you. If someone celebrates you or recognizes you for something this week, really let it soak into your body.

Celebrate it all, my love!

Chapter 3: Hitting Burnout

Sitting on the cold, hard floor, mostly in a closet is where I would suffer silently through anxiety attacks.

For my earlier lives I think they disguised themselves as asthma attacks, but as I got older, I got better at hiding anxiety attacks. Burnout came on like a freight train. When you spend your life in a never ending cycle of: it's never enough, go-go-go, do all the things and always saying yes, you begin to feel stretched thin.

That's honestly how I felt most of my life. Thin, stretched, never enough. I would constantly achieve, say yes, and do things that weren't lighting me up to make other people around me happy. I would fill my days with things to do, organizations, jobs, sports, activities, because deep down I didn't want to sit and feel my emotions. I didn't want to have to dive deeper. What if I got stuck there, I would ask myself? What if people didn't think I was positive if I was having a bad day? What if it slowed me down?

Of course I didn't realize this was what was happening as I was growing up. I'm an Aries. I have a lot of fire and success energy inside of me. I wanted to succeed, I am very driven, but also some of it came from a place of fear, a place where I *have* to do this. I put a lot of internal pressure on myself.

In High School I was hit hard with Mono. I was even in the hospital because of the pain I was feeling from an enlarged spleen. This began my journey with Chronic Fatigue Syndrome.

I would feel highs and lows of energy throughout college, graduate school, throughout when I was working full time, and even in my beginning years of entrepreneurship. I wasn't honoring my body. I was still forcing, still pushing through, still avoiding. I was told to slow down so often and in reality, nothing in me wanted to slow down. Slowing down did not feel safe in my body. I had dreams, passions, a place I needed to get to now. There was no time for "rest" in my eyes.

It wasn't until I left my full time job and began my entrepreneurial journey that I was slowing down and speeding up at the same time. It was then, I realized I was going through adrenal fatigue. Mix this in with bikini competitions, diets, and years of disordered eating that I hid from others and you can start to get the picture.

Once I decided to get healthy the right way, things began to change. When I was able to slow down, rest, not pack my schedule every second of the day, life shifted. I dive deeper into this in the Body Image and Burnout Chapter. This was a whole new realm to enter.

We're set up societally, generationally, historically to burn out. We're praised for how much we can do in our jobs, how much we can take on, how little we can rest and keep going. I remember in the education world, it would be a one-upping party of who was the most exhausted, who stayed the latest, endless amounts of venti coffees from Starbucks and pressure to answer emails within minutes that came in.

Talk about nervous system overload!

So many experience burnout because from the top-down, we are wired for it. We're wired for it from a lack of attunement and regulation of our systems, from a lack of boundaries, and a lack of prioritizing rest.

Rest for most, especially for those from low-income or BBIPOC backgrounds, isn't a place that is safe. We aren't shown healthy rest, we definitely aren't celebrated for resting. Often, resting is met with laziness, the constant belief that we need to be on and doing something, or the extreme feelings of guilt.

Guilt. How guilty have you felt when taking a break, taking a day off, or even taking a week off of work? Guilt for taking time away from family, loved ones, friends? Guilt for when you need alone time, guilt for when you say no?

Often experienced in our phases of rest, relaxation, or being is the "waiting for the other shoe to drop syndrome" - where we are unconsciously in our bodies scanning for something bad to happen. It might show up as:

"What if something bad happens when I'm away?"

"Who am I to take this rest?"

"I can't possible receive and relax"

"Good things come but they don't stay"

Also, it might even not pop up as conscious thoughts, but as a physical sensation in the body. It may come through as anxiety, constriction, racing heart, the list goes on and on. You may not even notice the sensations as I share this and your sensations may look different than how I'm describing them. This is happening from unconscious blueprints and past attachment traumas.

Our bodies hold a well-being set point. I learned this from two of my mentors, Andrew and Peter. When things are going good our bodies can only handle so much goodness, then it starts to become unknown. We may not feel like we can keep it, create it, that it will last, that it's safe for it to stay, that we could make it happen again.

We may unconsciously self-sabotage or not let ourselves truly enjoy the experience of it because we've lived in the past of good things coming in and good things leaving. If that's been the norm for you, or you've experienced this in your life, you may resonate with what I am saying. The more we allow ourselves to soak in the well-being that we receive, opening up our heart centers and tap into our receiving energy, to anchor in those moments, to allow ourselves to be held, supported, to rest & receive, we begin to collect drops and sips of this energy that gets stored and rewired in our systems.

Most don't notice burnout in the earlier stages of it. We notice it when we are at a breaking point and everyone's breaking point looks different, so it's important not to compare yourself and your needs to others. Whether it's work related burnout, relationship burnout, life burnout, it doesn't need justification or an explanation. It's your truth and no one can take that away from you.

General Signs of Burnout:

- Feeling anxious with all there is to do and accomplish off a to-do list - yet adding more
- Lack of boundaries and fear of setting boundaries
- Feeling as if there is never enough, never being enough
- Placating to get through the days
- Coping via numbing activities (phone scrolling, food behaviors, alcohol)
- Lack of energy or concentration

The list goes on and on. I'm also not a professional in the realm of burnout medically, but rather just sharing my experiences in how this impacted me on an energetic standpoint and an emotionally healing state.

Working with burnout requires a top down and a bottom up approach to the work. What does that even mean?

We live a lot of our day to day in our minds and we are trying to think our way through our emotions and how to feel better, rather than feeling the sensation and being with the emotion as it pops up in the physical body. We try to use conscious mindset work (affirmations, changing habits and thoughts) to heal.

While those things are great, they aren't getting to the root cause of the work, they are like band aids with a bigger problem happening underneath. We have to work with where it began as a root. We also have to connect into the felt-sense and sensation in the body. Some of these symptoms and experiences of burnout also live in our body so we must work with the conscious, the unconscious, and the body to begin to re-wire and re-write the pathways to healing. In doing this, there's an opportunity to bring in compassion.

It's not judging the sensation, trying to make meaning out of it, or fixing it. You're not broken and shoulding on yourself won't bring in the change from a place of love. Hold yourself through what's coming up, honor the sensation, experience it, and bring compassion to it. It's probably been waiting for you to see it, hold it, and love it for so so long.

See if the ego & the mind can drop out of the story, the how, the why, the way, the doing and see if it can just be and let the body do the work.

———

Have you ever tried to pull a big plant out of the ground?

You grip both hands around it tightly.

You pull with all your might.

Fall on your ass.

Dig the shovel around it.

Pull again.

Fall on your ass.

Get a bigger shovel.

Pull again.

Fall on your ass.

You take a little break and think.

Okay this time this fucking thing is gonna come out of here.

Fail.

You start to realize the roots of this thing are deeper than you thought.

So you ask the person next to you, can you try to get this?

They pull it out easy.

You laugh.

Of course this always happens. (You know when something won't open or turn on, it always works when someone else does it)

There's a few thoughts here:

1. Our outcome won't change with just trying different tools. You can hope and learn that the next tool will be the thing, but the thing is - it starts with the roots. Your roots are your beliefs. If you want the plant to rebloom you must repot the soil, safely. You have to be willing to do the deep work to see the massive results. To untangle those roots and see what else they are connected to. Where did these stem from and where else is this a pattern in my life?

2. Transformational work ain't a walk on the beach. It's gonna require you to look some deep stuff in the eye.

3. It's sustainability for your business and life to grow. It'll often feel like you got sucked into a wormhole and shot back out like what. just happened.

4. It forces you to shed. Shed the new identities, new beliefs, new feelings, new everything.

5. Not everything requires force to work. What would your life experience look like with flow?

6. We aren't meant to do it alone. We can't see it ourselves. Someone else will open up the light for you.

In this work, lies the next level version of you.

If you're wondering why aren't I "there yet"

Then it's time you start here.

Untangling the roots.

INTEGRATION & EMBODIMENT:

This chapter's integration exercise is to two fold.

First, take inventory of where you might be experiencing some symptoms of burnout in your life. The list in the chapter may be a beautiful place to guide you on what is coming through for you. You might make it a three column chart. First, writing out where you're experiencing burnout, what it feels like (either emotionally or physically), what needs to shift (maybe it's a boundary or a conversation for example, or even just being with the emotion) and what the desired end result will be from the action.

Second, start a daily practice (even better if it's a few times a day) to bring awareness to the physical sensations happening in your body. See if you can be with the sensation, allow it, witness it and hold it from a place of love and compassion. Honor it for what's coming through. See if it has a need, if it is protecting you from something, if there is something it wants from you or for you.

Chapter 4: Playing Small Owning your Shit & Stepping into your Power

Playing small kept me safe. It kept me from disappointment.

Even when I had the deepest of desires, I wouldn't let myself edge past what I really wanted. I would go one step "safer" so I know I could achieve it and wouldn't be let down. It was a protector of mine.

Developmental disappointment is an indicator of attachment trauma (Peter Cummings). Throughout my life there were times I would feel massive disappointment. So to protect myself from the constant pain, hurt, and disappointment - I kept myself small.

People would say to me: "you don't show a lot of emotion, you're so quiet." You're one of those pretty "even either way people," as if it was a bad thing. I just couldn't get myself to fully be present in any moment because my mind was racing to protect me: "what's next Erin, there's more to do, more to heal, more to earn, more to help." A constant running pattern of what's next?

Another word used to describe me: humble. Which yes, is a good thing to some degree, but not when it's used as a protector from not being able to receive success, compliments, and joys.

Instantly always in denial, pushing away the love, whatever I could do, because I just couldn't let it in. It wasn't safe for these things to stay. I believe our ability to receive is a dance. We need to allow ourselves to let in the good, to let in the well-being, and also some healthy ego is okay too!

If I didn't rock the boat, make anyone mad at me, then I had nothing to worry about. My body would physically shut down, if I made someone upset. Cue little Erin who would follow my mom around asking if she was mad at me when really my girlfriend just needed 5 minutes to go to the bathroom alone.

I played small in many areas of my life so I wouldn't get my hopes up. I held back what I wanted to say so I didn't have to get let down, and also so people wouldn't leave me. I had a deep fear of abandonment, of people leaving, saying something bad about me, so I just placated to make sure everyone was happy. But everyone was happy at the expense of myself.

I thought I had to follow the rules, be the person at my old jobs who said yes at the expense of myself, and hold back my truth. Placating, playing small, and holding back your deepest desires is a precursor to burnout. So check in with yourself. Ask, am I holding back from speaking my truth, from playing all out in my life and what I want for myself, and really getting clear on my desired outcome?

One day, I said fuck that. Actually, it wasn't a day, it was a culmination of deeply healing myself and standing firm into boundaries, owning my shit, and stepping into my power. Ther was no fucking way I was going to keep going through life like this. None.

Another note, so many often play small and hold back in a fear of being seen. Unconsciously, being seen might come with having attention on you, or taking away from the attention of others. It might have opened you up to criticism, other's thoughts, and uncomfortable vulnerability.

The body can go into a receiving or being seen overload and there's so many reasons why some don't want to be seen. It could have been in the past that when they got attention, it hurt others, or they were told children are better seen and not heard. The list is truly endless of why playing small and holding ourselves back feels more safe in the body. If you ever had to walk on egg-shells at home or take in others experiences, you may find yourself in a pattern of playing small in life.

———

Let's talk next about owning your shit.

We're quick to pass off owning our shit. For me, owning your shit means owning who the fuck you are and what you are here to do in this world (with the deepest of integrity, please). How many times has someone said to you, "Oh my gosh you are amazing at this" or some other form of compliment and you brushed it off. Nah, it's no big deal. Just like when someone compliments your dress and you say, "Oh I got it at Target, I don't really love how it looks, but it has pockets."

Take the compliment. Own your shit.

Own the transformation and the magic you are here to make this world. If you're good at your work, celebrate yourself and be excited and so proud of you! Obviously, some healthy ego is needed. I'm not saying be an egotistical asshole, but damn, we need a new paradigm of owning who the fuck we are.

Own all parts of you!

What if you embraced all that you were?
The sweet.
The sensual.

The fire.

The wild side.

The healer.

The divine feminine.

The divine masculine.

The CEO.

The partner.

The lover.

The coach.

The mystic.

The goddess.

The wild womxn.

The kink.

The visionary.

The evolving.

The one who has massive dreams.

The one who allows nothing to hold her back.

Fuck the rules, the boxes, the shoulds.

It's time to emerge into where you desire to be.

To be met & held so deeply in every area in which you are wanting to receive.

There's no room to play small or hold back what's meant to be yours.

Your expansion is calling.

Your bigness is ready for you.

Step into your Power!

In the breakthrough, we step deeply into our power. Stepping into our power doesn't mean powering over others. It means stepping into our divine power, our truth, or way, the essence of our being.

It's saying, "F the shoulds, the boxes," the way other people tell you you need to be doing something, whether that's in life, business, or however this may be showing up for you right now.

I spent so long in my business following other people's way of being and how it worked for them. I thought if I could just do this "right" and follow this, it would work. Then I said, what if I let myself lead?

What actually feels good in my body? What's a hell yes or what's a hell no?

Ah, those sensations and checking in with myself changed my life. The spammy way of selling, lack of trauma-informed sales techniques, following the "status quo" and what all the other coaches and humans were doing to be successful felt like pure torture. So I leaned into my way, my truth, what felt good for me, and hey! Those things may work for other people, but we can't follow a cookie cutter strategy when we are all unique snowflakes.

We get into this lens of wanting to do things right. Often for most this can be a trauma response and a fear of something bad happening, if we do it wrong. I've seen it be paralyzing for some of my clients in not wanting to mess it up, do it wrong. Which is completely normal - when you've grown up in a household where you had to do things right to receive love, or maybe you always thought if you were perfect or did it right, you would stand out and be seen.

Remember, it's safe to embrace the messy action and to hold yourself in discomfort. If you weren't always celebrated for who you were, and for more of what you did, then this is your opportunity to see you for all those parts of you. To embrace the less perfect way and to find your ground of safety along the way.

Want to know what happened when I did this? My business started to explode a few years ago. I stepped into my own power and built my own table and stopped giving my power away to others and their way of being.

I led, I went first, and I'm proud of the way we're doing things over here in my business.

Remember, don't let anyone take your internal power away from you. Use your discernment, call your energy back to you, and even in the world of patriarchy and everything else in between, lead, do it differently, be the change. There is no wrong when it comes to your truth. At the end of the day, that is what we have - our truth.

Sometimes we get into a belief or a response, a fear of doing it wrong and it can paralyze us. Embrace the messiness of life, of the action you take. It's better to learn and grow along the way rather than to not take any action at all.

INTEGRATION & EMBODIMENT:

I invite you to reflect and ask yourself: How can I step into my power today?

Maybe it's:

- Making a decision that has been on your heart
- Saying yes, or saying no thank you
- Getting on live video
- Writing that post you've been meaning to write
- Sharing that piece of your story you know others are meant to hear
- Embodying your ripple effect
- Owning your magic
- Setting a boundary
- Selling your offer
- Owning your prices
- Increasing your prices

- Celebrating how far you've come
- Taking up space
- Allowing yourself to be seen

How can you fully express and invite in all the parts of you? What would it look like to start to bring forward one of those parts you hide back and let her explore?

Chapter 5: I Am Not A Doormat

I struggled with boundaries for a long time in my life. I was the person who could "do it all" and I wore that deeply like a badge of honor.

I said yes, when I wanted to say no, I would overgive, overextend myself, and stretch myself so thin to make sure everyone around me was happy.

When everyone else around me was happy, I could breathe. It felt safe. I wanted to make sure everyone's needs were met over my own. I was operating with crippling anxiety making sure everyone got what they wanted, but I was left feeling depleted.

It was hard to speak my truth in that too. I kept quiet, nodded, and smiled. Saying "no" or "I don't have space for that" felt so scary in my body.

I wasn't aware of how to set boundaries. I was struggling as a people pleaser. When healthy boundaries aren't modeled for us as children, we tend to navigate the world with very similar ones, or maybe we try to do the opposite in hopes to find control. This could be emotional boundaries or physical boundaries. My fear in not honoring my boundaries and speaking my truth in what I needed stemmed from a few things:

Knowing My Needs
Communicating them
Releasing the fear of abandonment
Not needing to meet them all myself

Knowing my needs. For most of my life, I would have told you I didn't really have many needs. Anything I needed, I could figure out and do by myself. I used to wear this like a badge of honor. I can do it, I can do it for you too. I would over-extend and give myself to others. I would try to set a time boundary, then would break it. In my business I tried to set money boundaries, then broke those too. Phone boundaries? Yep, didn't have them, didn't communicate them, didn't know what they were. When I started to get clear on what my needs were, my instant feeling was guilt. I felt guilty expressing my needs, getting clear on what they were, and honestly having the realization for the first time in my life it was safe for me to ask for what I needed and get met in that. That would lead me to the next steps: **communicating and allowing it in.**

Maybe for you, finding the needs are easy, but it's communicating them that is tough. You'll find in the next chapter, I was cheated on in pretty much every relationship that I was in. It's because I also didn't have healthy boundaries either. I said yes to things I wanted to say no to, and no to things I wanted to say yes to. The cycle ran through me over and over again until I had to learn that I had to stay true to me.

Communicating when someone crosses a boundary was tough in the beginning for me. I was afraid of making them upset, or even worse they would emotionally or physically abandon me. Releasing the fear of abandonment, after speaking those needs, came with practicing and holding myself.

It meant not re-arranging all my words, reading a text a million times, apologizing first, over-explaining myself, or anything else. I had to hold the little version of me over and over as I spoke for what I was and was not available for in life, business, relationships.

Some honored this, and some didn't. I had to learn to be okay with that, which isn't always easy for the past people-pleaser here. Strong and healthy boundaries = less burnout. That is the truth.

Allowing others to hold you and respect you in your boundaries can be an edge. Trust me, I get it. There will be times too when others don't honor your boundaries and that's the next part of the exploration.

You get to stand in your power and speak up for your boundaries from an embodied place. You get to feel anger or whatever emotion comes through when your boundaries aren't honored and you get to speak up for you and them from a sacred place.
There may come times when people keep disrespecting your boundaries over and over again and then you're faced with bigger decisions.

Communicate your boundaries, honor them, and notice what happens if something isn't followed through on either your end of the boundary or on the receiving end.

There have been times when I've broken my own boundaries and have had to bring in an immense amount of compassion, forgiveness, and a review of what needs to happen moving forward. I can give myself grace and also hold a higher standard for myself to honor my boundaries. It's self-care to do so.

When others happen to break my boundaries, it's having an embodied conversation with that person. It's speaking my truth, communicating from a grounded place, and letting them know what hurt and didn't feel good in the process.

I believe it's helpful to share: how you feel, what the impact was, what was brought through emotionally and internally, and how to repair moving forward.

Sometimes the other person may not have realized it was a boundary break. We also have to be sure these people know our boundaries rather than mind-reading that they know our boundaries. This involves communication. It's honoring the part of us that might feel bad or scared when it's time to have that tough conversation, but at the end of the day, you have to honor you. If this boundary continues to be broken, then that is a deeper conversation and things that need to be considered.

Remember, don't ever settle or lose yourself in this process. You are worthy of having healthy boundaries in life, business, relationships and all aspects and that may be hard for others around you, especially if you are stepping into this maybe for this first time, or you are deepening them!

INTEGRATION & EMBODIMENT:

Take some time to review where you are feeling burnt out, overwhelmed, or feeling like a boundary needs to be set in different areas of your life. You might start with work/business boundaries, relationship boundaries, time boundaries, or phone boundaries.

For me, I can tell a boundary needs to be set when something feels off in my body. It sometimes pops up like I'm being stretched thin, resentment, anxiousness, overwhelm, or overload.

Start with getting clear on what those boundaries are, then you can decide which ones you want to implement first. Some say start with the ones that would have the biggest ripple effect, the one that feels like the one you can commit and follow through with, or the one that will get you some movement and feels like you can experience it and hold it safely. It might be a phone boundary first before a conversation with a friend. That might feel like the best place to start!

Start somewhere.

Don't forget to celebrate yourself and let your body see that you are getting clear on your boundaries and following through with them! This helps develop self-trust in the body and the body gets to see the impact.

Reflect: What does it feel like in my body when I set a boundary? What sensations might be present here? Is there a fear or belief that pops up when I set a boundary? Do I find myself care-taking other people's experiences rather than honoring my own needs?

Practice the communication aspect of setting boundaries. Even just saying it out loud before you have the conversation is so helpful! Use visualization to imagine the conversation going well and you standing in your truth.

Take time to decompress after. It may feel like a lot as you are starting to set boundaries so having time to honor yourself after and calm your nervous system is so helpful.

Chapter 6: Dating, Relationships & Sex

I would like to dedicate this chapter to all my past partners and thank them for allowing me to get here.

Okay, okay, all jokes aside. I've learned and healed deeper from every breakup, relationship, and person I've dated.

Here's the thing. I spent way too much of my life being in relationships a lot longer than I should have. Again, that "yes girl" energy of being the one who never spoke up when something was bothering her in fear of making someone upset, came back a lot in my relationships.

It came back in the form of being cheated on, taken advantage of, and not having people show up for me like I needed them to. I can take some personal responsibility in that I never asked. I wanted them to read my mind. Pair that with some major burnout and operating in full on masculine mode and there was no place for my queen energy in a relationship.

I lived in full fear operating in "what if they leave," I need to "keep them" even though they are a major asshole. I send so much love to this version of Erin every day. I thought maybe if we had more sex, more this, if I was more that, they would stay. Again, doing everything I could to make them happy, when in reality, that sounded horrible and those past partners weren't meeting me halfway. (While I can look at this and share it from this perspective, I also didn't attract some of these experiences, but I can share my perspective on how I learned from this versus being stuck in completing the cycle).

I think in the spiritual world we get into this idea that we attract all of these "negative experiences" because of our vibration - which is a very toxic way of thinking. I didn't attract assholes because of my vibration, but there was an opportunity for me to learn from them, learn boundaries, honor my needs, and move forward to end the cycle. I hope that makes sense!

It wasn't until I was listening to Chris Harder's speech at a conference, I had a huge realization. He talked about the rocket ship once it takes off. A rocket ship has two seats in it and the rocketship can't keep coming back down to planet earth to save the people.

That was me. I subconsciously was trying to fix and save these boys thinking I could be the one to help them heal their own issues (cue, inner child wanting to do this too).

Newsflash, I could not.

However, my rocket ship had to stop coming back down to planet earth to save the people. They had to decide if they were joining me, or not. Boom, I was not available any more for settling.

To be honest. Sex for most of my relationships seemed like a massive chore. I didn't have the physical energy most of the time or the desire. It seemed more like a thing to check off the "to-do" list so it didn't turn into a fight of "we only have sex 3 times a week" blah blah blah. I get it, we all have needs, but if you are reading this, the approach in your communication is helpful too. Also, allowing your partner embody the queen & be in their feminine aspects, helps too, no matter how they identify.

I'm always quick to admit in the deepest seasons of my burnout, I felt more confident and liberated when I had a few (or a lot) of drinks before sex. It was in the moments I could fully let loose, be more expressed, be more sexually curious and let my guard down.

Vulnerability and intimacy during sex? Nah, I was so in my head about my body, pleasing the other, and disconnected from my body's needs I didn't know that sex isn't just about pleasing another. It's about pleasing you too, boo.

Healing work changed my entire life in sexuality & expression. I am grounded in my body now to ask for what I need, to explore safely and express my desires, to be playful, to be so honored in my temple and my physical body that I am not sitting there thinking to myself "why are we in this position when I can see this roll, or this part of my stomach or blah blah."

Finding a secure base in your attachment system, coming home to your body, your sovereignty - as a woman - will change your entire way of being. It starts with you going first, honoring you, and beginning to bring this energy in. Of course, please always be safe, use safe words, and use discernment.

Sex, for me now, is a beautiful place of being in pleasure, exploring things like kink, Tantra, deeper intimacy and connection. It comes with freedom, with expression, with more orgasms and more fun.

I remember when I first started learning about feminine energy. I wanted to laugh and cry all at the same time. Actually, I think I did. I realized how much I operated in a wounded masculine or wounded feminine space.

Before I continue, let's break down some of these terms if you are new to this topic.

Masculine & Feminine Energies

- Masculine and Feminine Energies are not sex or gender specific, anybody has both of these qualities

Divine Masculine

- The divine masculine holds a deep presence in the system. There's support, healthy discipline, strong boundaries, a sense of stability and security. There's honesty, a sense of being held, protection, and responsiveness.

Divine Feminine

- The divine feminine has this flow, ease, and effortlessness to it. There's an openness, a creativity, and a sense of surrender. The divine feminine properties are magnetic, strong, empathetic, and trusting in vulnerability.

Wounded Masculine

- The wounded masculine can be very controlling and unstable. It might pull back and avoid, or be too aggressive and pushy forward.

Wounded Feminine

- The wounded feminine can sometimes appear in a neediness, a co-dependent sort of energy, and insecure.

As I began to embody and heal my feminine, so I could step into my divine feminine energy, so much began to happen in my life. I began to attract things with more ease. I felt less of a need to "do" to receive and more of a sense of "being" to receive.

Manifesting what it is you desire:

When I became single after a 6 year relationship back in 2018, I decided I was going to focus on manifesting the person I wanted to come into my life next by becoming an energetic match for them and focusing on myself.

So, I decided: what would I love to feel, experience, and be in a relationship with when it comes to the other person? Let me begin to give that to myself first.

This began my journey of dating myself. Each week, I would buy myself flowers, take myself out on dates, make myself coffee in bed, leave myself love notes, the list goes on and on.

I began to embody the energy of what it is I wanted in a partnership. Not just the physical things that would happen, or that this person would do - but how they would also show up for me emotionally too. I began to ask myself: what's it feel like as I'm receiving and allowing this in? Am I even open for it? I found myself in a place of holding back a lot, not asking for what it was I needed in relationships, friendships, etc. but the truth was, I had a shell around my heart that desired to be more open.

Inside of this deeper journey to loving me, I found an inner home, an inner peace. I stopped chasing a man to make me feel things that I needed to learn to create within myself. I dated myself, had the best time and enjoyed going out on dates too.

When we learn to receive from self, receive from others, and receive from a group - magic happens.

There's edges in each of these areas that we get to explore.

For me, the story was it was easy to receive from myself. I could lean into my own dating process, take time to meet my own needs, and be perfectly fine with me. Receiving from another and allowing someone to support me, to be there for me, to let me receive - was my first edge. From there, receiving from a group was the next edge.

This looked like opening myself up to be supported in groups which therefore allowed me to bring more people into my coaching spaces, cause I work through the parts that feel safe in holding and allowing more in and others to support me, rather than being the one to hold everyone.

Orgasmic Manifestation and exploring deeper into the world of sexuality, kink, and pleasure without shame opened up my world. I believe deeply that we are disconnected so much from our bodies because we live in the mind space that pleasure is sometimes hard to receive. We want to think our way through our old programming which makes it difficult for us to actually enjoy pleasure. There's so much societal shame in sexually expressed women and that needs to die in this old paradigm.

Exploring what feels good to you is your birthright. It's your birthright to explore your own body sexually, to live a life that's turned on. Being turned on isn't always just using a vibrator or having sex. It's the way you move through life. From how fast you shave your legs, while brushing your teeth, and drinking your coffee while sprinting out the door with wet hair - to exploring the present moment, slowing down, tasting the pleasure of your food, the wind on your face, the sunshine on your skin. It brings you to the present moment. This is orgasmic manifestation.

I have many articles, posts, and information about this in my program, but I can tell you leaning into this energy skyrocketed my ability to manifest love, money, and opportunities in life.

Exploring your sexual desires and how you want to express yourself has also been a key piece in my healing in sexuality. For so long I felt a lot of shame around this, wondering if it was too much, keeping myself covered, and feeling guilt. Your desires are meant for you because they are yours.

There's endless shame in sexuality from different backgrounds, how you grew up, or what you were told about sex in school, etc. We are mostly taught sex is bad, don't have it and there is a lot of fear in it, so we feel shame for exploring what our bodies naturally want to do in seeking pleasure. Pause here and take a moment on what you've been told around sex, your body, expression, desires your entire life. Were you modeled and talked to about sex healthily, or was it a hush-hush conversation?

Finding liberation, healing the body based pressure, permission, exploration and slowing down in all the doing in my life healed so much of relationship with pleasure. When I look back, I realize how disconnected I was from my body. When I didn't feel comfortable in my own skin, I didn't want to connect with a partner. When I was working 16+ hour days, there was no time in my head for pleasure. When I wasn't allowing myself to fully receive pleasure and be pleased because it didn't feel good to just be and receive, I wasn't wanting any sexual encounters. When I could fully express myself without needing a couple drinks to feel liberated, my entire life began to change.

INTEGRATION & EMBODIMENT:

I want to invite you to take yourself on a date, or even plan a sensual date night in for yourself. Maybe it's going out to a restaurant and buying yourself a nice dinner. Maybe it's cooking, drinking a glass of sparkling water (or wine) while you make yourself a bomb dinner, a bubble bath, and a night in with your vibrator. Whatever it is for you, make it a vibe, and make it happen more often.

The second integration exercise is to bring your awareness to how much you are rushing through life. Trust me, I get that sometimes we are shuffling children and managing careers, on day 14 of dry shampoo and personal appointments all at once. I'll invite you, though, to bring in opportunities to slow down, to tap into the present, to use your senses to notice what's around you and to anchor into the deepest gratitude.

Thank you, more please.

Chapter 7: Money & the Art of Receiving

One of my biggest burnout to breakthrough moments was understanding and developing a positive relationship with money.

Some of my first money mindset work was understanding what I had been told about money, how my family viewed money, the stories and beliefs that were wrapped up in wealth, abundance, the people who had it and didn't have it. There was a lot of identifying in these beliefs. Money doesn't grow on trees, you have to work hard to earn more, hiding things about finances and not sharing openly about them, money shame, the list goes on and on.

If you're newer to money mindset work, I'll invite you to pause and just take a quick inventory on your beliefs around money. What were you told about money growing up? What are your current beliefs around money? How do you feel in your body with your relationship with money? How do you honor or not honor money? Do you find yourself shaming that there isn't enough, that debt is bad, that you should be "further along." What does that look like for you?

If you've been doing money mindset work for a while, there's a deeper level in the space that I want to invite you into. You may have re-programmed a lot of your conscious beliefs around money.

While this is amazing, we can't just affirm ourselves to no end, reframe all of our thoughts constantly, "just decide" and expect POOF all of our money beliefs will be fixed and cured. This is unfortunately taught a lot in certain spaces and then what happens is we get frustrated and stuck feeling that we are doing something wrong in our money mindset work and that we need to do more money-mindset work to increase and improve our wealth.

If you've done a lot of money mindset work, you're probably thinking to yourself, I've heard I should think positive, open myself up to receive, I have reframed my beliefs, I have decided, now what the fuck, universe. What else "should" I be doing?

The body and the unconscious have to begin to get on board and connect into what is happening in your body around money.

We often aren't even aware of the internal and unconscious programming and somatic memories that are stored in the body when it comes to money.

There are two different forms of memory: Implicit and Explicit. Implicit memory is your unconscious memory, or procedural memory. This may include the emotions present at a situation and your body or physiological responses. Your explicit memory (conscious memory or declarative memory) remembers the facts of a situation. It may remember the time, who was there, what happened, and so on (Somatic Experiencing, 2021). Think about this in relationship to rewiring your money beliefs.

Some of these may be stored in your body, in your physiological response to money, and you may have no conscious connection to what is happening. So just affirmationing yourself, journaling for days on end, might not even bring up the unconscious and the somatic memories stored in the body.

There may be years of generational trauma around money or even receiving support. There may be pre-verbal, or memories in the womb that happened for you around money or receiving support. It's not always the relationship to money itself, but our connection with receiving support, nourishment, being taken care of, and asking for support. The list goes on and on here.

Implicit memory is a real thing. It may not make conscious sense because it doesn't require conscious attention to encode this in your body. It may just be the way we move, the way we operate, the way we respond to receiving money, support, connection, etc. Trauma can be passed down 7 generations linearly so even if a great-great-great grandparent had to deal with feast and famine during the great depression for example, you may have those programs running in your body. When you heal this, it changes the lineage both forwards and backwards.

We are deeply connected into this belief system that we have to do more to receive. Being to receive doesn't always feel safe, or realistic.

For many (and to add especially if you identify in a marginalized population), there wasn't a model of be, relax, and receive. It was to be scanning for what could happen next, be thinking about what else you can do, and it activates a deep response of survival. While your conscious mind might not be thinking "food, water, shelter, survive, don't get eaten by a tiger," - your body might be.

I remember even after doing years of money mindset work, two distinct memories that I can connect my body, changed the trajectory for me.

The first one was going to get groceries. I had plenty of money in my bank account to cover groceries and I said some abundance blessing over my receipt afterwards, but couldn't figure out why I still felt terrified. So I decided to experiment. There was a bodily response of my card declining or not having enough as I approached the register (even though there was enough) because of things that have happened in the past. I tracked a sensation in my body that was tightening and bracing as I approached the register. After taking a moment to hold the sensation and bring a sense of safety to it, I asked the clerk if I could just walk up again. It was a whole new experience as my body physically shifted. I make sure to honor this part when I approach to pay and remind myself that I am safe.

The second one was times I am paying my bills and having a money date. I would consciously say out loud all my gratitude, appreciation, and celebration, but internally my body was still going "are we going to be okay?" "do we have enough?" Wow. I thought to myself, there's a deep survival fear here. Even though my conscious mind was knowing there was safety and that things were taken care of, my body was scanning and parts were getting activated. I had to hold those parts of me and truly honor the body in the process.

The third time wasn't actually even related to money, but being to receive. I was laying on the couch with a whole free Saturday. I had a list of things that needed to get done, but really wanted to honor myself and chill. I repeated over and over to myself that it was safe to rest, safe to chill, safe to be. Again, my body was going oh no. It didn't feel safe in my body for me to rest. My mind was scanning for something to do. I couldn't rest in "being" because my body wanted to be doing. It felt so much safer to be doing than to truly be relaxing and receiving.

Receiving connection and support is something that I deepen my relationship with every day because there are so many layers. As someone who used to do it all by herself and took so much pride in that, I've had to find safety in my body and a settling in allowing connection, allowing support, and truly working with my nervous system when it's time to relax and rest that it's more than okay to do so. I orient myself a lot into my spaces and into transition time to get my body to connect into myself.

This brings me to the next section of this: Operating in the Highs & The Lows and the Chase.

For me, and many of my clients we find this addiction to the chase, to the getting, to the next level. We are programmed that at the next "level" we will be safe, things will change, and that something will be different. While yes, with more money comes more options to maybe buy some more things, invest, etc. - we are searching for this external validation and a feeling of safety, support, that we think will come from this next level. We become addicted unconsciously to the chase, the next thing, thinking "This" will be the thing that changes everything.

Operating in the highs and in the lows in life, especially with money - was the normal for me. It's what I saw happening throughout my life. Large sums of money would come in, then I would be back to over-drafting. I would pay off a bunch of my credit cards, just to be back maxing them out again. This wasn't honestly a spending issue for me. I wasn't going out and buying tons of clothes, bags, etc. and not that there was anything wrong with that, but it was frustrating to me to figure out why I was always ending up in this up again and down again space.

Then it hit me, this is what felt safe. This is what I knew. I had to burn out in order to break through. Digging myself out of something gave me a high when I came out of it. I felt strong, I felt worthy, I felt like I could do this.

I was praised for it throughout my life too. I would battle some major sickness, injuries, accidents and was praised for my strength of being able to get through anything. Unconsciously, I knew highs and lows, how to operate in them, and getting out of it was "validation" for me.

I began to understand how to truly support my nervous system in the highs and the lows, as ups and downs in our income, in life, in business are very normal things. I had to be able to hold myself in those moments, not make meaning of it that it was good or bad, or that I was doing something wrong. Compassion had to come in to regulate myself and pull myself out of the stories that I was back *here* again.

You can truly never go backwards if you are healing and moving forward in your life, but it sure felt like it so many times when I ran the same pattern.

Our life and healing journey happens in layers and little pieces pop up for us to dive deeper, and guess what, we are always healing it from a new foundation. We are always healing it from a new layer and a new level. As we stabilize our systems, we increase feeling safe in holding more, in allowing more. It increases our energetic capacity to receive more.

We all have a set point in this. There will be a point where it almost feels *too good* to be true. Again, we might not be thinking this consciously, but our body responds to our set point. Sometimes when we hit our set point, we might have the thoughts of: "How will I do this again", or feeling as if we are waiting for the other shoe to drop, or we might unconsciously self-sabotage.

I've had this when hitting some of my highest income months. My bank account was in over-flow, I had more than just enough, I was receiving deep intimacy in my relationships, beautiful friendships and my body went "oh fuck". We've been desiring this for so long, what if it doesn't stay? What if it leaves?

I saw a lot of that pattern in my life, masculine leaves. The steadiness and sturdiness I felt in this felt amazing, I was high on life, and inside my body still had a point of, what if it doesn't come back? Cue abandonment type wounds, worthiness, and my well-being set point. Instead of judging myself here, I could lovingly hold myself.

I had a part triggered that it was going to get left behind. I invited it to come along with me in the growth. I reminded my body it was safe to hold and allow more in, and that I wouldn't lose it, that I wouldn't have to do more.

This is a process and a constant commitment. You can't just snap your fingers and this belief is instantly shifted. It's a constant connection, dedication, and investment to yourself. You can't just think to yourself I want more abundance, I want 10k months. If your body doesn't feel regulated in going there, you'll cockblock yourself.

Or, you might get there and feel out of alignment, anxiety, or something else because the body doesn't know how to sustainably adapt to this. A reminder here to stop comparing yourself to others who you feel that are "further" along than you. Check in with yourself. Are these people running a business in a way you want to run yours, is their lifestyle supportive, is their business model sustainable?

Especially as women. The more women who are deep in integrity with the work they are doing and are making an impact, deserve to receive more. This was a huge shift in my body as I truly stepped into the CEO role in my business. Most of my time in my earlier stages of business, and honestly all of my life, I operated in just enough. Just enough to pay all my bills, just enough time to maybe find a moment to breathe in the day, just enough in relationships.

Don't ever fucking settle my love. You're worthy of overflow. You're worthy of more than just enough, so don't just ask for "just enough" in your relationships, in your job, in your business, in any area of life. Desire and shift your being for overflow. It's one thing to receive all of this, then allow yourself to practice keeping it, having it, and re-creating it. It's not a one and done type of situation, find the safety and certainty in consistency. In longevity. It's safe to trust you.

I realized I didn't trust myself a lot with money and abundance. I was too burnt out and strapped thin to realize I shamed myself, shoulded on myself, and felt guilt. I tried to heal myself from this place that something must be wrong, something must need to be fixed, and that I had to be broken or running a pattern that wasn't serving me.

You can't heal from an energy of shame or should. We heal from an energy of love, compassion, support, and gentleness, and the magic happens. So pause and ask, where are you being hard on yourself and telling yourself: you should be further along, you should be making more, have more saved, be married, have the kids, be at the certain level in your job. Instead, ask yourself how can you honor and celebrate yourself for where you're at right now and then you can create your next level desires from this place?

I brought in a lot of that shame and should energy when it came to my relationship with debt. You're talking to the girl who went all in on her business and continues to everyday. I invested in myself when the money wasn't there yet, used credit cards, pulled my 401k. I was a resourceful little nugget with a big ass dream.

I can admit I made some of those decisions from a un-regulated system (didn't know any better at the time) - there will be times in life when we stretch ourselves, but we have to feel safety in our bodies as we stretch and be able to lovingly hold ourselves in those holy fucking shit moments.

I saw my debt as this emergency. I had to get rid of it, I had to pay it off, oh no, there's more, it's piling up, my income isn't growing, I need to do more to pay it off.

Debt is not an emergency. Yes, it's good to pay it off, desire financial freedom, that's not what I am saying here. I'm saying, are you so focused on getting out of debt that you are deeply restricting yourself, or building your business to just get out of it thinking that you will feel differently? It's a huge accomplishment to be debt-free don't get me wrong! But pay yourself first, save, find safety in having good debt. Find a different energy to scale from rather than a pressure of just paying off the debt because society says that is what it means to be financially free.

I've had huge connections in my relationship with food and my relationship with money. It operated in the highs and lows too. I would restrict, binge, purge with food and would restrict, binge, purge with money too. This was a never-ending cycle of burnout and perfection.

I would want to restrict my money via shame, then get to a place where I needed to put it all towards my debt to get rid of it. I focused on, "just make more money" and that will solve my problems. It didn't. It just created more of maxing myself out at a higher income rate.

Peter Cummings, one of my mentors, teaches that one of the four cornerstones of a secure attachment is a balanced pacing with money and food. So yes, part of my healing in this was diving deep into healing my attachment system and finding a pacing.

Operating in the Linear vs. the Infinity

I love this concept when speaking about the energetics of money.

When we begin to play in the realm of the infinity with abundance, love, ease, money, whatever it might be for you, so much can begin to happen.

Sometimes, our internal pressure comes online.

What if it doesn't come back?

I need this to work.

We judge our past self and predict the future based on past experiences.

We'll think:

What if it doesn't work out?

What if I lose it?

When this happens then I will..

We often play in the realm of the linear.

When our next level is infinite.

Linear thinking looks like: I need to do more to receive. If I put x amount of time in, I should receive x. It may look like a fear of letting go of money in fear that it may not come back. It may be thinking when this happens, then I will.

We want to lean into the infinity of money. Money isn't linear - it's energy and it's an infinite resource. This may look like trusting and surrendering to receive. Understanding that money circulates when we release it and it always comes back to us tenfold. It's playing with quantum energy and asking ourselves what if it does work out? It's knowing we go first and the universe responds to us.

Pause. How's your body doing right now? Check in with any sensations that may be present as I'm going to move into sharing about attachment styles next.
I share deeply about attachment styles in a lot of the training I do. Attachment theory from Bowlby and Ainsworth is taught in the concept of relationships, however, our money is also a relationship.

So think about how you would want a partner to treat you and how you treat a partner. Judging, shaming, and being needy to it, isn't a good feeling, but lovingly supporting it and nurturing it is a healthy way for a relationship to grow.

Below I will break down a few of the main attachment styles and how I personally relate them into our relationship with money.

Anxious Attachment Style with Money:

- It may feel like a never enough energy, or a fear of it running out even when there is a state of overflow
- Operating pay-period to pay-period or finding yourself always being strapped for cash
- Anxiousness might come online if someone doesn't want to work with you, or says no
- Fear when there are slower months that it will never come back or you're doing something wrong, shame might set in
- Emotionally escaping with money, possibly a judgment that it isn't here yet, isn't coming fast enough.
- Reviewing money and bank accounts constantly from an anxious energy

Avoidant Attachment with Money

- Feeling the high highs and low low's with money, this may be a high income month to a low one, or a lot of ups and downs in relationship with money

- An energy of push and pull, wanting to be supported by money, and also terrified to actually have it come in and meet the needs
- Consciously or Unconsciously avoiding money by blowing it off (maybe avoiding looking at bank statements, bills, getting the mail) or avoiding messages in the DM's of people wanting to work with you in fear that you might get rejected
- Keeping the cravings for your desires at an arm's length (i'll leave you before you leave me, so you can't get hurt or disappointed)
- Not having strong wealth-care or money management principles

Anxious/Avoidant

- If you find yourself feeling a little bit of both categories with money, you may fall a little under this category. We don't want to identify with "I am anxious" "I am avoidant" but honoring the parts of us that are activated and bringing into a secure base.

So what's a secure attachment with money look like?

- Money and months can fluctuate, there may be months that are higher and dips, but there isn't an alarming feeling of "oh no, I messed up or did something wrong" the person can lovingly review and see where change can be made.
- Not looping into a spiral if someone doesn't want to work with you, or if a client payment is late.
- Can have open and honest money conversations and feels secure in this conversation.
- Healthy sales energy and doesn't feel a need to be pushy or bring through masculine/lack of trauma-informed sales practices to earn a sale. More to come on this in my next book.
- Has strong boundaries with money, healthy practices, checks in with money via money dates and can notice when something may get triggered in their relationship with money.
- Knows that money won't bring in external validation and that must come from within.

Beginning to work to heal our attachment styles is a much deeper conversation than I am going to go into in this book, but awareness is key. So start there and notice what comes up for you in your relationship with money (or personal relationships). Feel into the emotion and take a moment and pause and hold yourself in it, then take the awareness into action from there.

INTEGRATION & EMBODIMENT:

I invite you to schedule a money date this week! Money dates are a vibey experience where you can get intimate and connect with your money. I like to light abundance candles, have a glass of wine or a sparkling beverage, and review all my finances, goals, and play energetically with what I want to receive and where I desire to go.

Also take inventory of what you feel in your body with your relationship with money.

I remember so many days sitting and staring with anxiety at my bank account.

I'm going to overdraft again: Cue anxiety, shame, judgement. Investments were going into my business on already maxed out credit cards, cue spiraling thoughts of what if I don't make this back right away?

But what I realized most and what I realize in my clients is it isn't always our relationship to our money specifically - but the energy and frequency we have connected to other feelings in our life we have that can match the flow of money, rooting in our safety, our security.

I did the same thing with food. I would binge and purge. It didn't feel safe for it to stay and I received an emotional charge from "digging" myself out every month of my financial situation. The moment I "made it through" I felt enough, accomplished, worthy, safe. I kept recreating those situations because that's how I was getting a lot of those feelings.

We have to begin creating those experiences in our bodies now.

We have to allow ourselves to heal the guilt, shame, release the judgment.

Remembering: You are safe, held, secure.

It's safe for money to stay.

You're worthy of overflow.

You are enough & that money is a beautiful amplification.

Experience full gratitude, celebration, and honoring of all abundance.

Anchor in anytime you are receiving.

Honoring your little girl who might have felt similar feelings in what is going on with money & meet her need that she is desiring from you.

Ask yourself: what's the emotional charge more money is going to bring to you and begin to bring that to yourself now?

Here's a few ways you can begin to honor your receiving energy:

1. When given a compliment: Thank you, I receive that.
2. Asking someone you trust: I really need some support right now, do you have space to help me with this?
3. Begin to notice where you DO receive: money, support, love, and celebrate it.
4. If someone says "can i help you with that" allow yourself to receive it.
5. Notice what it feels like in your body to receive: place your hand over your heart or wherever you feel the sensation and anchor in this magic:
6. Take messy action: what can you release that isn't perfect or doesn't need to have it "all together?"

Chapter 8: Decision Energy

I believe that breakthroughs come from a consistent and strong decision energy.

I spent a lot of my life in a place of saying yes and figuring out the details afterwards. It was no different from when I decided to write this book. I said yes to a big goal, dream, and vision then had to figure it out along the way. It was no different from when I started my coaching business, when I pivoted in my business multiple times - you get the point. All of this came from a decision, a little bit of jump and the net will appear, mixed in with hope, faith, and trust.

The energy from which we decide, is what shifted for me as the years went on. When I would first make a lot of decisions in my business and life, it was from a rocky foundation. I would definitely jump without a net, but I was jumping from a foundation that wasn't built on safety in my body and a deep trust in myself. I had a knowing and trust in myself, yes, but there were many times I jumped from a dis-regulated nervous system. There was a lot of fear, a lot of worry, a lot of what if's that came in my decision making process. Which trust me, I get is so normal when you are running a business, but there is a difference between, oh fuck - I don't actually have a foundation of safety and healed trauma in my body, vs. oh fuck - we are doing this, I am shitting my pants, but I trust me so deeply and my system is regulated.

Lets chat about unconscious roots and how they might be holding you back in business, life, and relationships.

We often run programming of inconsistencies in our life in our attachment to our businesses. This can be rooted from an inconsistent parent or caregiver in childhood, or experiences that weren't fulfilled or needs met in the way they needed met. Inconsistency in our businesses often feels "normal" when we grew up with emotional instability at home.

You might be thinking "my home wasn't really that unstable" but even emotions being unpredictable (hot/cold, good mood/bad mood), or being met in the way you needed to, can run this out in business, partnerships, etc. Obviously our parents did the best they could with what they knew, but even those missed experiences or needs being met in the way your templating needed them, can create this anxiousness or avoidant tendencies in our businesses.

How it shows up in business or romantic partnerships:

It can almost make us thrive on unpredictability and instability in our businesses (unconsciously of course). For some, it's most of what we have known, so it weirdly feels "safe" and normal for our systems. We know how to operate in the ups and downs, and stability, reliability feels weird.

Then we feel a need to perform, do, hustle, work hard, go. We reach a high, it feels good, then it doesn't feel safe to keep it. Again, on an unconscious level. So truly being in overflow, having ALL of our needs met, without something running out, not being met is like WTF.

When we find it hard to make decisions in our business, there's a lot from childhood that can be tied in here too. It may be a lack of trust in the self, or being honored in the "achievement" as a child rather than identity and being.

For most, we were celebrated and honored on what we did, rather than who we were being. Rest, self-care, identity, isn't as celebrated compared to achievements, etc.

Gas lighting can definitely be a factor in this too. If the family adopts a discrediting of what you do, how you do it, if it goes against what the family does, etc. Or if you made decisions and they didn't follow the "right" thing that your caregivers or parents wanted you to do or what you "should" be doing.

Example: "why would you leave your full-time job? You'll lose your 401k and health insurance!" "You should be saving your money, don't carry debt!"

How it shows up in business:

Should I do this, should I not?

There may be a lack of safety in small or big decision making.

Indecisiveness, circling a lot in decisions.

Deciding without a safe foundation.

Shoulding on self for where you aren't yet.

Constant need to be doing (lack of safety in the being).

"Being" doesn't feel as supported or celebrated.

Showing up & then going back into recluse mode.

There are many different roots, causes, and outcomes for how this may have started & where it might be showing up in business, but it's something for you to think about and to begin to bring your awareness to.

This is why:

- Reparenting and parts work is very needed.
- Safety & Healing and connecting into our bodies, unconscious mind and nervous system is game changing.

We can trust ourselves, feel safe in our decisions, ride the flows of entrepreneurship, enjoy ease, safety, and presence.

Decisions aren't always going to be easy, either. I think we all know this. Something that is talked about a lot in the online and spiritual spaces is if something is hard, it must be out of alignment. To be honest, I don't agree with this. There's going to be decisions, things in life, business, relationships, that don't feel good from a place of resistance.

Maybe it's something that you don't enjoy doing and you aren't in a place to outsource it yet. Maybe there are growing pains in your healing work that you are working through and there's hard conversations that are happening, boundaries that are being set, the list goes on.

There's a deep difference between being out of alignment and it's a fuck no in your body, vs. working your way through resistance. This is why learning to get into your body and navigating your body based cues is so important. I'll give you some tips in the integration section to help you navigate how to make decisions from a grounded place.

We must also break the conditioning of making constant head based decisions that are rooted in logic. I believe in quantum leaps and quantum leaps don't always come from calculated decisions. They come from a knowing in your body, a deep trust in yourself, a stretching "oh shit can I do this" and a deep surrender.

We are conditioned to make very logical decisions in our life. My past logical decisions led me to burnout, and my quantum beliefs in fuck the rules, I don't want what makes sense, led me to massive breakthroughs.

We are conditioned to go to school, get a good job, pay off debts, get married, have a family. Don't get me wrong, those are all amazing things and should be celebrated! However, if you're just following that route to make someone happy, to do it because that is what you are supposed to do, or whatever society says...my question is why?

No matter what route you are following, are you doing it because someone says you should do your business in xyz, run your relationship in a certain way, or are you letting your intuition, your dreams, the shit that doesn't make sense lead you there?

I can tell you it didn't make sense when I left my full-time job to go all in with my business, to leave relationships that weren't serving me, to say yes to a big vision, to move away from a small-town in Ohio, and all the other decisions I made. However, I know that I am here for the next level things that make zero sense, so here we are.

Make decisions from your next level version of you, yes, and also make sure you aren't stretching yourself so thin that you are so overwhelmed, and fearful of whether it's going to work or not, that you can't enjoy the ride.

We can stretch our comfort zone, encounter the ride, without going way too over the deep end. This goes for how we support others in making decisions too!

You'll read more about this in my second book: The New Paradigm of Selling, but I wanted to bring a little bit of the magic here to you now to help you in the Burnout to Breakthrough.

How do you support your clients in making decisions, or friends/partners if you aren't in the online coaching space but have stumbled over this book? Do you make them respond to you on your terms, do you encourage them to just do it, to say yes to be in the energy, or are you helping them make decisions from a grounded place? Help them to regulate and honor their decision making process.

THIS is what changes the collective.

Be a leader, dare to do it differently.

INTEGRATION & EMBODIMENT:

So, if you are reading this and you are like many of my clients who then ask me, "how?" - let's talk about how to trust thyself and make decisions from a place of safety.

- *What is the belief or fear that is coming up for me in this moment?*
- *Is this fear an illusion or is it truth?*
- *Have I experienced this distrust in my past? (Be with that experience and take a moment to hold yourself in that)*
- *Where can I collect evidence that it DID work out, or that I took action in another area of my life?*
- *Where energetically can I take action and create and establish trust within myself today?*
- *Bring through celebration and recognition for the subconscious.*

Another tool to use to help to understand how you make decisions is human design. I'm by no means an expert in human design, but in the Energetics of

Business Podcast, my friends Lauren and Neha and I share about how understanding your authority can help you to know your decision making process.

Getting into your body and being with what is coming up for you and honoring it is the best way to regulate yourself before making a decision.

For me: this looks like:

Awareness of the situation: example: Investing in myself or my business.

Awareness of the thoughts & body sensations: mind is going oh shit, can we do this, will it work out? Body is feeling: tightness, constriction, survival mode on.

Place my hand on the body sensation and bring an energy of compassion to it. The mental part is a protector to the body sensation, so we will often have to work with that too. How can I feel safe in this? Accessing and orienting to safety for the body, letting the sensation move through, and collecting evidence for my unconscious mind. After I feel regulated, then I can make the decision.

It doesn't mean I'm still not like "oh shit, here we go" but then my decisions are coming from an aligned place versus when my body is in a response.

The more I began to regulate myself throughout the day, trust myself, leaned into support, allowed myself to be held and stopped with the pressure - decisions have become so much easier.

You can still be a decisive boss CEO and take time to regulate your system. Let's break the paradigm of, "if you don't decide in 2.5 seconds without asking questions that you aren't decisive," shall we?

Chapter 9: Body Image & Burnout

I spent most of my life at war with my body.

From an early age my doctor called me thunder thighs. I remember throughout elementary school being aware of my "chubbiness as I called it", weighing myself on a scale, and comparing myself to those around me. This comparison of my body was one of the biggest factors that contributed to my burnout.

I remember after eating pizza in sixth grade, going to the bathroom to make myself throw it up. At the time, this seemed like a logical idea. Eat the food you want to eat, make yourself throw half of it up. I would go on to repeat this cycle throughout points in high school, but mostly college. College is when this became more of not a random couple time a year thing, but a daily practice sometimes for months, and then it would stop again.

I was competing for the Miss Ohio competition and started going down the spiral of binging and purging everything I ate. I also lived on lean cuisine meals, 100 calorie pack snacks, too many nights of cranberry vodkas, and endless hours on a cardio machine at the rec center in college.

I loved the compliments of wow, you look amazing! What are you doing? What was I doing? Slowly killing my body and hiding the fact I didn't know why I was having kidney infections, UTI's, and panic attacks in my room.

On the outside, I had it all together. It was a beautiful protector for me. Even the closest people to me would have no idea that I was struggling so deeply inside with my body image & feeling enough. So I continued in a cycle of over-working, over-involving, and putting on a smile to make sure that no one could know this deep dark secret that I was holding inside.

I stopped this cycle when I moved to Florida. I decided in my mind, this is not going to be helpful to me anymore. I need to begin again. This is my new start. I need to get healthy the right way. I then started a journey of clean eating, lifting weights, doing at home workouts, and of course after you end disordered eating: weight gain.

I thought to myself: well I am not doing these unhealthy things anymore, I've cured my eating disorder. Little did I know, just ending a pattern isn't healing the deep rooted issue of it.

From there, I decided to do a figure competition. Which if you know anything about bikini competitions, outside of the spray tan, giant water bottle, and bronze trophy - it's hell. I decided to do this in grad school and while I was proud of my determination, the cycle coming after it was also hell. Your body can't sustain that size and physique for longer than like oh, a day. So began another journey of loving my body, honoring it, supporting it, and finding balance.

I spent years after that as a health and fitness coach, helping women and men find a balance of the foods they loved and creating a sustainable lifestyle. However, it didn't matter how many meal plans, workouts, and plans I made - a health & fitness journey is so much deeper than that. I think a lot of people focus on the conscious changes and forget to address the deep rooted programs that are going on.

So let's address some of my learnings here since you have a little bit of my story.

The number on the scale, the way you look in a photo, whatever that is for you, is you searching for a false sense of security. Fuck. I remember having this realization and not even having a clue what it truly meant, but knowing it hit me in the soul.

What I realized was the unconscious belief that my body, the way I looked, allowed me a sense of control and through this vessel I could find a sense of safety and control. If I just leaned out here, if I could just grow my booty, if I could just lose 5lbs. Bullshit Erin.

What are you actually searching for in this? You're saying it "doesn't matter" but it did. I was hoping in this that I would find a deep sense of worth, of feeling safe in my body. However, your external body can't create the safety of what needs to happen in your body. You have to go inwards. You have to understand your attachment patterns, the traumas, because here you are still picking apart your body.

What a fucking ride that healing journey it has been. What I came to discover was I didn't fully feel safe in my own body. Going back to my reflections of being able to "be" and "allow" couldn't happen because I searched on a journey to fulfill some void that could never be fulfilled.

I searched for my shell to try to protect me from what I was avoiding inside. I had a false sense of security. Until I began to create it within me, to heal the trauma responses, to learn how to truly hold myself through what was coming up for me, did the magic happen.

I'm so proud of myself now in this aspect of my journey. I'm the heaviest I've been, but the most balanced, and healthiest. To also preference here, if you're on a journey to lose weight, sculpt your body, or whatever that is, that's amazing! Always ask yourself though, for what purpose, what's the intention? Is it to truly be healthy or is it to look a certain way to prove something to yourself?

Again, nothing is good or bad or wrong or right, my thoughts are always to find what energy & intention your goals are from. My journey now is for health & fulfillment. I lift weights, enjoy pizza, give myself grace & compassion. Compassion is a bitch sometimes isn't it? We live in a world of should-ing on ourselves. A place of comparison, a place of judgment for where we used to be.

Our unconscious mind loves to collect evidence. The unconscious mind actually has many prime directives. It wants to keep you safe, it loves to serve you, and wants to prove you right. What does that mean? When you're shifting into a new place in your journey, a new goal, a new way of being or doing something scary and new it'll say: wait, this didn't work out before, activate: keep her safe. We have to begin to collect evidence from other areas of lives where maybe things have worked out, where things were easy, where change has happened.

Prime Directives of the Unconscious Mind + Body

(Information from Quantum Ripple Effect ™

Coaching & Healing Certification

1. Preserves the body

2. Runs the body - Has a blueprint of body as it is now, and of the body in perfect health

3. Stores memories - Temporal (in relationship to time) and atemporal (not in relationship to time)

4. Is the domain of the emotions along with the body

5. Organizes memories along with the body - Uses a Gestalt on the timeline

6. Represses memories with unresolved negative emotions

7. Presents repressed memories for resolution

8. Is symbolic - Uses and responds to symbols

9. Takes everything personally

10. Works on the principle of least effort - Takes the path of least resistance

11. Does not process negatives - Don't think of a blue tree, you still have to think of a blue tree

12. May keep the repressed emotions expressed for protection

13. Is a highly moral part of you - The morality you were taught and accepted

14. Enjoys serving, needs clear orders to follow

15. Controls and maintains all perceptions - Both regular and telepathic, and transmits them to the conscious mind

16. Generates, stores, distributes and transmits all "energy"

17. Maintains instincts and generates habits

18. Needs repetition until a habit is installed (the quicker, the better)

19. Is programmed to continually seek more and more

20. Functions best as a whole integrated unit

INTEGRATION & EMBODIMENT:

Notice what your current thoughts and beliefs are around your body.

How are you consciously or unconsciously connected to your body? Do you find yourself scanning your body in the mirror, doing body checks often, what are your habits and reflections with your body?

One embodiment practice I love is mirror work. I love sitting or standing in front of the mirror and touching my body, sending it love, gratitude, and energy. I thank it for all it does for me. I honor it daily.

Something else that helps me when I'm having moments with my body is breathing or tapping.

To note, these embodiment practices came after years of deep healing work with my body, so it's easier for me now to release. These are also not ways to cure anything, but again my experiences that have been helpful along the way.

Chapter 10: Celebration & Fully Expressed

Celebration was never something that felt easy to me for most of my life.

To be quite honest, it wasn't something I was consciously aware of that I wasn't doing. I had programmed myself to always be onto the next thing. One of the prime directives (duties) of our unconscious mind is to always keep us running to the next thing.

That's how I spent most of my life. What's next? What's the next thing I can achieve, the next thing to do, the next place to live.

I was so disconnected from the present moment. To be honest, until I began my healing journey - I couldn't remember a lot of memories from younger years. What I realized is I was dissociating and running a trauma response most of my life. Throughout my healing experience and the power of breathwork, attachment work, and somatic healing I have been able to connect and heal.

Celebration is an incredible form of gratitude. When we celebrate, we can anchor in the moment, the experience, the beauty of the present.

I spent a lot of time in my head, thinking my way through everything. As I discussed in the Hitting Burnout chapter, trying to logically think about our emotions versus actually feeling and being with them sends us in a constant spiral and doesn't address the deeper root of it.

Manifesting and calling in your desires begins with you feeling the energy of what it is you want before it even happens. What will you see, what will you hear, what will you feel when you have it? How can you begin to embody the energy of where you're going now?

Want a six figure business? How is she showing up and moving throughout her day?

Want a partner? How can you feel and create the experience of that person now?

Make the goal you're hitting, or desiring to hit, a big fucking deal. Celebrate every little step of the way as celebrating acts like a snowball. A snowball doesn't get built into a snowman until it gets bigger, but it starts with rolling one snowflake. Find a way to celebrate yourself, who you are, not just what you do, every single day. Celebrate your essence, celebrate your existence, celebrate your impact, your accomplishments. It all deserves to be celebrated.

I know for me celebrating was so difficult because it required two things: for me to truly see and honor and recognize myself, and what I thought was a lack of control. So my first question for you, is what is it like for you to fully see who you are? Who are you outside of your achievements? Who are you at your core and your essence? What is it that you love so deeply about yourself?

The second, what is it like for you to release control?

Can you surrender to the divine timing, or are you still here trying to grasp at your outcome?

We find ourselves in this space where we are trying to control the divine timing of what's meant to unfold.

Let's bring this in terms of business, your career, etc..

You have a big goal for your next launch, year, whatever, but you found yourself falling short.

Instantly, you make it a *you* thing.

What am I doing wrong?
Why am I falling short?
Why isn't this happening at the rate I desire it to?

There's a part you're trying to control to feel safe.

To find a false sense of validation in your goal.

There's this beautiful thing called divine timing.

And yes, you have to put in the work, the healing, obviously - this isn't a sit back and hope it happens kinda energy.

But can you enjoy the journey?

The ride on the way to what's already yours?

Can you surrender into the quantum field?

Can you trust yourself enough to know that no matter what, you'll keep going?

Can you let yourself be held and supported on the way there?

Can you keep showing up for it consistently without judgement, without resentment, without guilt, or know that when those things come up, that you can hold and regulate yourself during it.

How can you attune yourself to your business?

To meet it how it needs to be held?

Judging/shaming/pushing it isn't supportive to the growth.

imagine if it was a child?

How can you bring it compassion, expansion, and lovingly support it as it grows?

The unknown. A place that can bring up so much fear and also so much potentiality. Can you hold yourself in that fear and also expand into what's possible?

Lean into your goals and where you desire to go. On our path to our goals, know that we don't have to always be efforting our way there. This connects into and plays out the idea that it has to be hard to achieve our goals, and while yes, there's work to be done, not everything has to be a push pull.

We can scale and achieve our goals sustainably with quantum leaps when we aren't just focused on the conscious changes that need to happen. The logical levels of change show that environment and behavior are at the bottom. So often we are focused on changing our environment and behavior. We are working here in the conscious level only & efforting our way more in.

Ever said you were going to do something and then a few weeks in...you're back to your old ways & the motivation is gone? It's because we are only working with the bottom two levels here of environment and change. The magic happens when we make that change on an identity level. Working deep within the subconscious mind. We can't just change what we do. We have to change who we are being. This truly connects the mind, the body, the spirit together as one.

Fully Expressed

Allowing myself to become fully expressed in who I am, what my desires are, what my needs are and all parts of me has been one of the most liberating experiences.

I used to worry if I was too much, not enough, needed to be more or less of something or something else. Then I tapped into a healing of feeling whole, worthy, and honored myself for who I am, all the parts of me, every single day. We might have been told growing up we were too much, not enough, or somewhere in between and we shoved down those emotions, those needs, and those parts of ourselves along the years. Maybe we were afraid to upset someone, step on their toes, rock the boat. What if it felt safe to fully express who you were?

I know for me I worried about what others would say along the journey of my expression. What if a potential partner thought I was too much sexually, or what if I wasn't what they needed? I was so concerned again on if others were having their needs met versus feeling safe in fully expressing my own.

Fully expressing yourself is allowing yourself to hold your body in what might feel like shame at first, fear, guilt, or whatever emotion pops up. The more you can hold yourself in it, feel safe in expressing it, and allowing those parts to enter into your world, she comes alive. It's safe to have needs, desires, and to express yourself in every way your body needs. What does your fully liberated and expressed version of you look and feel like?

INTEGRATION & EMBODIMENT:

Reflect on who you are and how you can truly honor yourself in that? What aspects of yourself do you love? What would it feel like to activate the energy of your highest self and show up as her today?

I'll invite you too to get in touch with the parts of you, you want to explore or the parts of you you hold back. Begin to get curious about what the stigma is around these parts, or even what they might need to feel safe in fully expressing themselves?

Begin to safely express your needs and desires. Get clear on what they are and how your fully expressed version shows up. How can you allow her out to play this week and own all the parts of her? Take some time and journal out all the parts you are celebrating about yourself.

Chapter 11: The Breakthrough

What if there was nothing to prove?

What if your worthiness wasn't dependent upon how much you could do, how much you could receive, how much you could achieve? Our worthiness is inherent. I know for years I ran after a false sense of validation in thinking if I could just be, do, have more then something would shift. If I could just pay off all my debt, then I would feel safe and secure. If I could just heal this part of me, then I would have the love I desired, if I could just get to this income month, then (insert thing could happen).

When we don't fully allow ourselves to feel safe in the present, we chase. We chase external validation unconsciously in our minds and bodies to feel safe. To be quite honest, most people's lives and businesses are based on this trauma response. I know for so long, mine was. Everything in my life was built unconsciously to receive love, to feel enough. Of course I didn't think this with my conscious mind, but my body was unconsciously addicted to achieving, to the next level, to be love-bombed & to receive a pat on the back of "you're doing a good job."

I searched in my life for wanting to say things the right way, to wondering if I was doing it right, fearful of a misstep. A misstep had room for error, for negative feedback, a glimpse into my life that I didn't have it all together. What would people think if they saw that I didn't always have the answer, know what to do, know how to help, or know how to support? What would people think if I spoke my truth, said fuck the rules, and didn't play by what I was suppose to do?

Finally, I found the breakthrough. The breakthrough was that I didn't have to keep running this pattern of high and low or chasing the next thing to feel some sort of way. This. All of these states and energies could be created within me. When we heal our trauma, release what society deems as successful, we heal burnout. We heal the ever ending cycle of not enoughness. We stop making things mean something and we start coming home to our truth. We feel safe in asking for what our needs are and speaking up to get those needs met. We stop looking for something outside of ourselves to meet those needs and we learn how to bring them in, internally. We learn to self-regulate and attune ourselves. We get our adult version of ourselves online to our little child that lives in us that is needing to be properly held and taken care of so they can grow up and feel safe in this world.

The breakthrough is that you're worthy, right now. You're enough. Hustling from a place of needing to prove something isn't the vibe. Working harder isn't a badge of honor and burning the candle on both ends doesn't make you more successful. Living for the next thing, the next cross-off-the-list, will not bring you validation. Yes, we celebrate those things, we have healthy goals, we fucking rise as women and break down the status quo, but not for anything other than we get to. It gets to be easy, we don't have to always **burn out to break through,** and when the divine feminine rises, we heal the toxic culture.

Remember this. It's safe to ask for a break. It's safe to rest. It's safe to be and receive.

If you're finding yourself in a cycle of needing to do more in life, love, business, or receive more to feel a certain feeling, I invite you to pause. I invite you to take a moment and find safety in your body and in this place. You're safe here.

Never Settle.
Never settle for just enough.
Never settle for I can't, I shouldn't..
Never settle for less than what you desire.

Keep Going.
When it makes zero sense.
When it doesn't look like it's not going to happen.
When you feel the frustration.
When your intuition is nudging.
When people say to "be realistic"
When your purpose & passion continues to light up.

Set your SOUL on fire every single day.

Because this gift, this idea, this message, this vision, wouldn't be given to you if you didn't have the ability to fulfill it.

It might get hard sometimes, you might have to get resourceful, you might feel frustrated, you might have months where you question it, you might feel like you've been at this forever now, but guess what.

The breakthrough is coming.
Your desires are planted.

Life is too short to waste time on your what if's...

because what if it all does work out?

I love you.

Integration:

Get clear on what your needs are. What are your needs from yourself, what are your needs from your partner or family, what are your needs from your career?

What sensations are present in your body when you rest? Do you feel safe to rest or is there something your body wants to do to feel safe?

Do you find yourself being praised for how much you can handle at work, or are you looking for validation in how much you have going on? What would it look like to celebrate rest? What can you begin to outsource off your plate to make more space for living?

The Ending

Here I am in tears. The end of my first book. Since I was a little girl I would write stories. I wrote short stories, plays, and poems. I minored in English and was the person who enjoyed reading and writing papers. I believe words are healing. The energy we can feel in our bodies from reading, learning, and witnessing, changes the game.

I invite you to take a deep breath. You're alive. There's so much to celebrate at this moment. The energy of your highest self, your quantum field, your whole potentiality surrounds you. Maybe it's cliche, but life is too short not to be, do, and have the things you want to create.

So maybe it's time for you to honor you deeper.

To leave the job.
To have the conversation.
To start or end the relationship.

To go all in.

To trust yourself.

To take big leaps.

To celebrate you for everything in life.

To say I love you.

What do you want the next 1 year, 5 years, 10 years to look like for you? It takes one small shift, one small breakthrough.

Thank you, my beautiful soul, for being here. I appreciate you trusting me with your time, your energy, your space, your eyeballs, and your heart for reading this book.

As you know, this book is based on integration. It's based on not just learning, but integrating and embodying on a deeper level. For less than $30 you can purchase my burnout to breakthrough mini program, a series of guided meditations, breathwork, hypnosis, EFT tapping, and healing to guide you deeper into your journey of getting into your body, healing burnout, and having your next breakthrough.

My vision is to ripple this book out to the masses, if you loved the book, tag me on your instagram stories @erinnicolecoaching or post it on facebook and tag me "Erin Nicole Porter" or "Erin Nicole Coaching."

www.instagram.com/erinnicolecoaching
www.erinnicolecoaching.com/breakthrough

If you are interested in becoming a coach, you can check out my internationally board accredited program: The Quantum Ripple Effect. In this program you become a board certified coach in NLP, Hypnosis, EFT, Time Techniques™, Life & Success Coaching, Reiki, and the Quantum Ripple Effect Methodology.

https://erinnicolecoaching.mykajabi.com/quantum-ripple-effect

Made in the USA
Middletown, DE
18 September 2023

38626131R00096